Audacious EXPANSION

Breaking Free
FROM LIMITATIONS TO
CREATE YOUR ULTIMATE LIFE

ERIKA ROTHENBERGER

burning soul press

Hardcover ISBN: 978-1-964924-31-1
Paperback ISBN: 978-1-964924-49-6
eBook ISBN: 978-1-964924-32-8

"This book is for the woman who knows she's made for more but feels like fear has her on lockdown. It's for the leader who wants to show up more authentically, not just climb another rung on the ladder. It's for the mother who's tired of being told she has to 'balance it all' and is ready to create integration that feels right. It's for anyone who's ever been knocked down by life and wondered if they'd ever get back up again."

-Amberly Lago, USA Bestselling Author of "Joy Through the Journey," and "True Grit and Grace" Top 1% Podcast Host, TEDx Speaker, Coach

"What makes *Audacious Expansion* so different is Erika's ability to blend raw vulnerability with actionable strategies. She reminds us that setbacks are really setups in disguise, and that true expansion isn't about doing more—it's about being more. Her words challenged me to rethink my comfort zone and start building my legacy today. If you're brave enough to begin, this book will guide you to your next level."

-Kathryn Gordon CEO of The Jon Gordon Companies, Founder of Gordon Publishing

"Erika's story is raw, real, and exactly what women need to hear right now. *Audacious Expansion* is not another hustle-harder book, it's a guide to leading, living, and showing up with more courage and authenticity. She proves that setbacks really can be setups in disguise. If you're ready to stop shrinking and start owning your power, this book will move you."

-Barb Betts, CEO, Keynote Speaker, Relationships are Your Superpower™ Podcast Host

"I met Erika at a women's conference in Spring 2025 and was immediately captivated by her magnetic energy and presence. Watching her audaciously leave her mark on the world as a national keynote speaker, podcaster, and mompreneur inspired me deeply. Reading *Audacious Expansion* felt like Erika was speaking directly to me—boldly reminding me that my limitations are not my destiny. This book is more than words on a page; it's a mirror reflecting the possibilities that open when we dare to step beyond fear. Every woman needs this book in her library as a daily reminder that true audacity isn't always found in the big leaps but it's cultivated in the tiny, intentional moments when we choose authenticity over approval and courage over comfort."

-Dr. Cheryl Wood International Empowerment Speaker, 2x TEDx Speaker, Best-Selling Author, Founder of SpeakerCon and Global Speakers University (GSU)

"The words 'audacity' and 'audacious' are becoming overused, often by people who like the sound of the words but have not lived an audacious life. Erika is the real deal. Over the years, I have been blown away by the combination of fearlessness and vulnerability in which she tells her gritty story. She's determined that her story not just be a gripping tale, but a transformative vehicle for leaders aspiring to own a functional level of boldness. Erika reminds us as she recounts a harrowing point of her story, "...every moment is a choice: live or give up." Boldness is also a choice, and it can be taught, which is what Erika does so powerfully here with her BOLD framework. This manifesto is for every female leader recovering from a setback or finally ready to move on from an era of small thinking. The boldness and the breakthrough you need are here."

-Jade Simmons International Speaker & Performer, CEO of Jade Media Global, Author of *Audacious Prayers for World Changers*

"Erika and I met because we're both national keynote speakers in the personal development space... and in one phone call I knew she was different. It was her ability to command a conversation while still leaving space for the other person to shine. Her vulnerability in turning her personal trauma into purpose. Her unique ability to turn the volume on life up to full blast. This is Erika, and this book teaches you how to show up just like her. I once told Erika that her energy shows up on a zoom before she does... that's how magical she is. If you want to learn how to walk through life with that same magic, the answer is in the pages of this book."

-Jamie Hess, Media Personality, TEDx and keynote speaker, and Coach

"*Audacious Expansion* is a guide that reminds us that growth isn't just about reaching higher, it's about going deeper into who we are meant to be. So many of the philosophies in this book mirror the way I've committed to live and lead with boldness, boundaries, and grace; honestly reading this felt like a validation for every woman building her own audacious life.

Erika's story and the tools she shares are going to awaken something fierce and freeing in everyone who turns these pages. This isn't just a book; it's a permission slip to expand beyond what you thought was possible. Erika's story is the reminder we all need that expansion isn't about doing more, it's about becoming more.

If you're building a big, audacious life, *Audacious Expansion* will meet you right where you are and remind you that your limitations are not your destiny. Erika's courage and wisdom make this book a love letter to every woman choosing to rise, rebuild, and lead herself forward."

-Kim Fitzpatrick Co-Founder of Lumina Legacy Institute, Co-Founder of Fitzlife Co., Founder of Legacy By Kim, Author of "Be Her Now" and Co-Host of the Fitzlife Unfiltered Podcast

Dedication

For the wild ones, the dreamers, the doers—anyone brave enough to crack this book open and expand audaciously.

To Andrew, my husband — my ride-or-die, dream-backer, and steady force when life gets chaotic. You never flinch at the crazy ideas. You just say, "Go."

And to Drew and Adelyn — my forever why and greatest gifts in life. May these pages remind you that legacy isn't built someday — it's built daily, boldly, with love and grit. I wrote this for you. I'm audaciously proud to be your mom.

GRIT GRACE & GLITZ PODCAST

THE AUDACIOUS BOOTCAMP MASTERMIND

AUDACIOUS WOMEN'S SUMMIT

Letter to the Reader:

Hey you,

Can I tell you something? I'm sitting here writing this, wondering what brought you to this book. Maybe you're feeling stuck. Maybe you're tired of playing small. Maybe someone handed this to you and said, "You need to read this." (Bless them.)

Whatever your reason, I'm so glad you're here.

Here's the thing—I've read lots of books that made me feel inspired for about twenty-two minutes before I went right back to my same old patterns. (Sound familiar?) And I thought, what if we did this differently? What if instead of just talking about change, we actually... you know... *changed* things?

That's why this book is built differently. Yes, I'm going to share my stories—the messy ones, the painful ones, the "I can't believe I'm telling you this" ones. But more importantly, I'm going to give you real things to *do* with what you learn.

You'll find **Audacity in Action Challenges** throughout—these are your steps toward transformation. Some will feel easy. Others might make you want to hide under a blanket. (Pro tip: the blanket-hiding ones are usually the most important.)

There are also **Share Your Journey** prompts because, honestly, this journey is so much easier when you're not doing it alone. These give you the exact words to share your progress and connect with others who get it.

Look, I know you're busy. I know your to-do list is longer than your Amazon order history. You don't have to do every single thing I suggest. But maybe, just maybe, you could try the ones that make your heart race a little? The ones that feel scary-exciting instead of just scary?

And if you're like me and need to dig a little deeper before diving into action (hello, my fellow overthinkers), scan the QR code below to access complimentary journal prompts that'll help you process what you're learning and get clear on what you actually want to change.

Sometimes the most audacious thing you can do is pause long enough to figure out what you actually want—not what everyone else wants for you, not what looks good on paper, but what makes your soul say "YES, this."

This whole thing? It's messy. It's imperfect. It's going to look different for you than it does for me or your best friend or that woman on Instagram who seems to have it all figured out. And that's exactly how it should be.

Are you ready to see what happens when you stop waiting for permission and start giving it to yourself?

I'm here for it. And I'm here for you.

WOOT, WOOT! Let's go,

Erika L. Rothenberger

Foreword

by Amberly Lago, USA Bestselling Author of "Joy Through the Journey," and "True Grit and Grace" Top 1% Podcast Host, TEDx Speaker, Coach

When I first met Erika a few years ago, I was instantly drawn to her passion, her big heart, and—let's be honest—her audaciousness. I swear she must have a secret closet filled with superhero capes, because the way she shows up for her family, her career, and her community is nothing short of extraordinary. Erika isn't just someone who talks about courage—she lives it, breathes it, and embodies it in a way that makes you want to rise higher, dig deeper, and expand more boldly in your own life.

I've been in the speaking and leadership world long enough to know that many people share good ideas, but only a few have the ability to move you to action. Erika is one of those rare people. What drew me to her wasn't just her story—it was her authenticity. She doesn't lead from a polished pedestal; she leads from the trenches, from lived experience. She has known trauma, setbacks, and the kind of pain that could have silenced her. Instead, she chose to transform it into purpose, creating a message that is both relatable and revolutionary. That's why, when she asked me to write this foreword, I didn't hesitate for a moment.

What makes Erika so compelling isn't only her resilience but also the scope of her impact. She's a civil engineer and executive who carved a path in one of the most male-dominated industries out there. She's a keynote speaker, podcaster, wellness entrepreneur, and mom who shows us that you don't have to shrink any part of who you are to succeed—you can expand. She's also proof that leadership doesn't mean doing it all alone. Her frameworks, like the BOLD Method and the Triangle Principle, aren't just strategies—they're roadmaps for building a life that's aligned, abundant, and sustainable.

We are living in a world that glorifies hustle—where burnout is worn like a badge of honor and "busy" is the default answer to, "How are you doing?" Erika flips that script. She teaches us to replace "busy" with "abundant," to stop waiting for the perfect moment to start, and to embrace what she calls the "Starting Line Mindset." These aren't just catchy phrases—they're lifelines for anyone who has ever felt stuck, overwhelmed, or unworthy of more.

This book is for the woman who knows she's made for more but feels like fear has her on lockdown. It's for the leader who wants to show up more authentically, not just climb another rung on the ladder. It's for the mother who's tired of being told she has to "balance it all" and is ready to create integration that feels right. It's for anyone who's ever been knocked down by life and wondered if they'd ever get back up again.

What sets this book apart is how directly it speaks to you—to the moments when life feels overwhelming, when fear keeps you from moving forward, or when you wonder if you'll ever feel "ready." If you've ever felt stuck, exhausted from chasing balance, or weighed down by setbacks that left you questioning your worth, this book meets you there. Instead of lofty theories or quick-fix motivation, it gives you real, actionable tools you can put into practice right away—frameworks like the 3-3-30 Method, the Audacious Badass List, and the Choice Points Journal. Each chapter invites you to stop playing small, to reframe the challenges in front of you, and to start expanding into a version of yourself that is not only stronger but also more authentic, more present, and more fulfilled.

Personally, what resonated with me most is her perspective that "setbacks are setups in disguise." That one truth has shifted how I look at my own journey, and I know it will do the same for you. Her courage to live out loud, to share both the grit and the grace of her story, is a gift. It's an invitation for each of us to stop playing small, to step into our own audacious expansion, and to remember that our limitations are not our destiny.

So here's my invitation to you, as you turn the page: don't just read this book—experience it. Take notes. Do the exercises. Try the tools. Let Erika's voice guide you as if she's right there cheering you on, reminding you that the cape you've been waiting for has been hanging in your own closet all along.

This is not just another book on growth—it's a call to action. If you're ready to stop hiding, stop hustling without purpose, and stop waiting for "someday," then prepare yourself. You're about to step into a journey of expansion that will change how you see yourself, your relationships, your work, and your future.

Your audacious life is waiting. The only question is—are you ready to begin?

Contents

Part 1:

THE EXPANSION AWAKENING

Don't forget to download your free journal before continuing.

Chapter 1:

PUNCH OR PIVOT

The moment you stop underestimating your worth is the moment everything begins to shift.

Have you ever had one of those mornings when you feel like you're on top of the freaking world? Like you might spontaneously break into a Beyoncé strut across the parking lot, blasting your own theme music in your head?

That was me. Middle of 2022.

I pulled into my usual spot at a suburban office building in Pennsylvania, slid my car into park, and looked in the mirror. I thought, "You know what? 2022 is looking pretty good, girl."

It felt like I was finally living audaciously by owning more of my true self than ever before. Pink heels in a male-dominated industry? Check. Thriving business? Check.

Family happy, kids flourishing, all the boxes ticked in my favorite planner? Check, check, and check.

I truly believed I was stepping into my boldest season yet. That little girl version of me—the one who dreamed of rocking a hard hat, running her own company, and leaving a giant, sparkly mark on the world—that dreamer felt alive in me that day.

I had my notes ready for my monthly VP meeting. I grabbed my beautifully color-coded planner (because obviously—*hello first-born, Type A Aries*) and my trusty Stanley mug filled with lukewarm water and a dash of Himalayan salt. (Don't judge me—an Instagram reel convinced me at midnight that it would make my skin glow like J.Lo's.)

I opened my car door.

And that's when I saw him.

A man I didn't recognize, standing way too close to my car.

"Sir, can I help you?" I asked, confused.

Five words. The last five words I spoke before a 210-pound stranger slammed his fist into my face, ripped me from my car by my hair, threw me onto the asphalt, and started punching me like a rag doll.

One punch. Then another. Then another. Blood, tears, and saliva dripping down my face.

In that chaos, my mind wasn't thinking clearly at all. It was pure survival—flashes of my kids' faces, fragments of "not like this," and some deep, animal instinct screaming "FIGHT,"

I wasn't having profound thoughts about being audacious or life lessons. I was desperately thinking: *My babies. My babies need their mom.*

Then his hands closed around my neck. Everything went black.

In that darkness, I had no idea this was the moment redefining everything I thought I knew about audacity. This wasn't about pink blazers and career goals anymore. This was about pure survival, raw strength—the kind that pulses from your bones when everything else is stripped away.

At some point, bright light hit my eyes. Somehow, from somewhere deep, I started crawling. Grip by grip, inch by inch, every movement a choice: live or give up.

I got to my feet and ran—still in those pink heels, every step screaming: *Not today. Not here. Not like this.*

After he failed to steal my car, he ran too.

I sprinted toward my office building, heart pounding like a drumline at halftime, praying someone would hear me. I burst through the doors and screamed—a primal, unfiltered scream that cut through the ordinary Thursday like a wrecking ball. Upstairs, vice presidents dropped what they were doing and ran toward the sound.

They rushed me to a trauma hospital. He was eventually found by dogs and drones as he tried to bury himself in the woods. In the ER, they told me he had a violent history—twelve prior years in prison, five women attacked before me, including a sexual assault.

In that moment, what didn't matter became crystal clear. Titles didn't matter. Dreams didn't matter. All I wanted was someone to put my face back together and tell me the world would stop spinning.

The next few days were a chaotic blur of police, detectives, reporters, and endless statements. So many moments I wanted to be "that" victim, to stay small, to disappear.

But then—I'd hear my kids' giggles in the backyard. The echoes of their joy felt like a lifeline, pulling me back to one decision: Would I let this moment define me? Or would I let it refine me?

Because when life punches you in the face—literally or metaphorically—those are your two choices. Let it define you, or let it refine you.

THE INVITATION TO EXPAND

They say trauma happens in slow motion. They're not wrong. But they don't tell you how it forces you to grow at warp speed.

My assault story is not about a random act of violence in a parking lot; it's about what happens in that split second when life demands more from you than you ever thought possible. It's about the moment when staying the same isn't an option anymore.

We've all been there in different ways. Maybe yours wasn't a physical punch. Maybe it was the quiet realization that you've been playing small for far too long. The relationship breakdown that forced you to rediscover yourself. The business failure that taught you more than success ever could. The loss that showed you how much love you were capable of holding. Or maybe it's happening right now, in a quiet crisis of purpose.

When we have pivotal moments in life, they snap us out of the mundane, the ordinary, the loops we fall into on autopilot. They force us to open our eyes and see where we really are, to look at the map we've been blindly following.

These moments—these catalysts—could just be challenges to overcome. Or they could be invitations to grow in ways you never imagined. Invitations to become audacious in your pursuit of expansion. To break free from every limitation and live your ultimate, wild, breathtaking life.

Every audacious move we make in our own expansion is a declaration of who we choose to be.

When you stop worrying about what everyone else is thinking, when you stop contorting yourself into shapes that please the crowd, you finally feel free enough to show up as your authentic, unstoppable, audacious self.

What I've recognized as I've gotten older is that I'm not going to be for everyone. And if I'm trying to be for everyone, I'm probably not being enough for me.

This is one of the hardest truths pivotal moments teach us—that trying to please everyone is a quiet form of self-betrayal.

We all have those voices in our head: "Today is not the day." "I'm not worthy." "I'm not ready." Those whispers that question our skill, our drive, our very right to take up space.

The real choice point is deciding which voice gets your loyalty.

When we're audacious—when we go after goals that matter, love more boldly, show up authentically, let limiting voices dissolve, and dare to risk it all—that's when true expansion begins.

But remember: even the strongest rubber band has a limit. You can stretch only so far before you snap.

The punch taught me that being audacious doesn't mean being all gas, no brakes, all the time. It means knowing when to pause, to breathe, to reflect—because sometimes you need to slow down to speed up.

YOUR EXPANSION BLUEPRINT

As you read this book, you'll discover how each chapter builds on these fundamental truths about audacious expansion. You'll learn to:

- Decode the pivotal moments that are actually invitations to expand
- Stop apologizing for wanting more and start claiming it
- Build your "audacity muscle" through daily acts of courage
- Create systems that sustain your growth instead of burning you out

- Turn your expansion into a ripple effect that lifts everyone around you

At the end of the day, how do you show up as the best version of yourself? The fully activated version? The you that will leave a legacy not defined by titles or possessions but by the energy you leave in the room and the lives you touch?

The punch that brought you to this book might be different from mine. But the choice is the same: Will you let it define you? Or will you let it refine you into someone more audacious, more expansive, and more alive than you ever thought possible?

AUDACITY IN ACTION CHALLENGE

This week, share one of your "punch" moments with someone who needs to hear they're not alone. Not to compare scars, but to show them what's possible on the other side.

SHARE YOUR JOURNEY

✺ "I choose to let my challenges refine me, not define me. What moment shaped you into who you are today? #AudaciousExpansion"

Chapter 2

GLOW UP, GORGEOUS (YES, YOU!)

The glow-up isn't about becoming someone new—it's about finally seeing who you were all along.

The year was 2001. Fresh out of college, standing in front of my cramped bathroom mirror, running my fingers along my hip bones, checking if they jutted out enough. Wrapping my hands around my waist, making sure they still touched. Counting ribs like they were milestones toward "good enough."

This was my ritual while struggling with an eating disorder—the daily check-in on just how small I could make myself, in every possible way.

When I look back at 2001 Erika, I hardly recognize her. That version believed she had to earn her spot in every room. She apologized for having opinions, yet felt parched for real connection and authenticity.

In construction, I spent years wearing gray and blue suits, practical shoes, trying to blend right in. I thought that's what it meant to be taken seriously in a male-dominated world. I thought if I shrank enough, they'd finally say, "She belongs here." Spoiler: they didn't.

Fast forward twenty-something years as I prepared to walk on stage to share my story with hundreds of people. I slipped into hot pink pants and traded my pale lip gloss for bright pink lipstick. I reached for sparkly boots in one hand and black pumps in the other. The question wasn't which one looked more professional or appropriate. The question was: which one felt like *me*?

I put on the boots. Obviously.

There I was—full volume, no filter, zero apologies.

During Q&A, no one asked about my slides. They asked about the boots. About courage. About being different. A few weeks later, a woman emailed me: *"I wore my red shoes to the board meeting today. Thank you for showing me I can be bold and still be respected."*

That's when it hit me: when one woman audaciously expands, she hands out permission slips to everyone else watching.

THE SMALL ACTS THAT CHANGE EVERYTHING

Here's what I know for damn sure: we put on masks to fit in, but we don't just hide from others—we bury ourselves. Every layer becomes a wall that keeps us from our own greatness.

And the more layers we pile on, the more we forget we were ever bright to begin with.

How many times have you bitten your tongue to keep the peace? Picked the "safe" outfit so no one would comment? Said yes when your entire body was screaming no? Dimmed your light so you wouldn't make someone else squint?

We tell ourselves we're protecting our reputation or relationships. But what we're really doing is suffocating our potential and robbing everyone around us of the full power of who we are.

True audacity isn't always about big leaps—quitting jobs, moving cross-country, launching businesses overnight. Often, it's quieter and far more powerful. It lives in those tiny, daily moments when you choose authenticity over approval:

- Saying no when your heart says no (trust those instincts!)
- Saying yes when your voice shakes
- Wearing what makes you feel alive instead of invisible
- Setting the boundary that terrifies you
- Resting when the world screams "push harder"
- Sharing that idea that keeps you up at night

These small, defiant choices add up to a revolution.

Audacious expansion can feel like a challenge because our brains are obsessed with belonging. Playing small fires up our amygdala—the fear center—whispering, "Stay safe.

Don't stand out." It's an ancient survival tactic that, in modern life, mostly just traps us.

Choosing expansion flips on our prefrontal cortex—the part that dreams big, solves problems, and dares to believe we can do more. That's where we come alive.

When I finally let myself show up in my full, raw, sparkly truth, everything changed. My team stepped up. My relationships deepened. My impact multiplied. Because authenticity isn't a luxury—it's oxygen.

Every single day, we get to turn the page. You don't erase your messy chapters—they're the backbone of your story, the ones that made you who you are today. The heartbreaks, the pivots, the rock bottoms? Those experiences are your raw material for greatness.

The thing you need to know about becoming unapologetically you is this: it pisses some people off. *Good*. You're not here to make everyone comfortable. You're here to make yourself proud.

The question isn't whether you're "audacious enough." The question is whether you're being fully, beautifully, relentlessly YOU.

Stop waiting for someone else's green light. Stop editing yourself down to bite-sized pieces that are easier for others to swallow. Stop apologizing for taking up space.

You know that voice in your head that whispers, "Who do you think you are?"

Here's my response (and I hope it's yours too): "I know exactly who I am. The question is—are you ready to meet her?"

This week, take one small, audacious step. Speak up when you'd usually stay quiet. Wear the thing that feels most like you. Say no to what drains you. Share that idea. Move toward that dream you keep saving for "later."

Because later isn't guaranteed. But right now? Right now is yours.

The world has been waiting for the unedited version of you long enough.

AUDACITY IN ACTION CHALLENGE

This week, choose one mask to take off. Start small—maybe it's wearing that bold outfit, saying what you actually think in a meeting, or finally taking a real lunch break. Write down what you learn about yourself when you show up more authentically.

SHARE YOUR JOURNEY

⊛ "Today I chose audacity over blending in. What small act of authenticity are you embracing?
#AudaciousExpansion"

Chapter 3

MIND THE GAP (AND THEN OBLITERATE IT)

*Unless you create action, unless you try to build that bridge
from where you are now to where you're going,
you'll never find your full direction.*

My husband Andy is almost four years older than me. Andy has always—and still does—teach me so much about being in the moment. When I can only see the dishes in the sink, he can dismiss them and recognize that it's extra time to spend at the dinner table in conversation. When I see the laundry basket overflowing, he reminds me that the kids will still go to school with clean clothes. How lucky I am that we have become the yin and yang that way in life.

I remember right before Andy turned 40, he looked at me and said something that stopped me cold: "I feel like something is missing."

At the time, I didn't get it. Honestly, I was pissed. We had two beautiful kids, we were living in what we thought was our forever home, and on paper, it looked like we had it all. I immediately made it about me. *Was I not enough? Was our life not enough?*

But what I didn't see then—and what I so clearly see now—is that he wasn't questioning our family or our life together. He was questioning himself. His purpose. That inner whisper asking, *Is this really it?*

He didn't have the words for it then, but he felt it—that quiet tug that so many of us feel at some point, wondering if we're truly living the way we want to be remembered. Years later, I understood. My only regret is that I didn't get it sooner. Because that feeling? It's not selfish. It's not ungrateful. It's a sign you're alive. It's an invitation to expand.

"I want more." Three small words that carry the weight of a wrecking ball. Not more stuff. Not more titles. More *life*. More alignment. More moments that make you feel fully alive.

You might be killing it on the outside. Corner office, dream house, Instagram-worthy family photos.

But inside, there's that whisper: *You're made for more.* That whisper doesn't always show up dramatically—sometimes it sneaks in as a quiet question, a gentle nudge, a moment that makes you stop and really *feel*.

Welcome to the gap. That space between who you are and who you know you could be. Between what you're doing and what you're truly capable of. Between existing and actually *living*.

It's that moment when you realize you've been sleepwalking through your own life. Going through the motions, checking the boxes, but feeling like you're watching someone else's movie play out on screen.

You know there's more brewing inside you—bigger dreams, bolder moves, a version of yourself that would absolutely blow your current mind. But somehow, you've gotten comfortable in the space between dreaming and doing. Between wanting and becoming.

It's cozy there, isn't it?

THE COST OF LIVING IN THE GAP

The gap is seductive. It whispers sweet lies: "You're not ready yet." "Wait until you have more experience." "Play it safe a little longer." "What if you fail?" "What if people think you're crazy?"

So you wait. And wait. And wait some more.

Meanwhile, life keeps happening around you. Opportunities come and go. Dreams get dustier. That voice inside gets quieter.

What I've learned about gaps is that they're not neutral spaces. Every single day you spend there costs you something.

Take *time*, for example. Time is one of our biggest assets, and yet it's the one we waste most freely without thinking twice.

We act like the things we know aren't quite right will be magically fixed in time, like wine gets better as it ages in a barrel. But unlike wine, our potential doesn't get better just sitting there. Each day in the gap is a day you can't get back.

Consider this reality check: You have 168 hours each week. About a third goes to sleep (and let's be real, most of us sacrifice that for "just one more email"). Another third goes to work. That leaves you with roughly 56 hours. The average person spends 17 of those hours scrolling social media. So now you're down to 39 hours each week to close your gaps—39 hours to move from existing to truly living.

And those 39 hours? They're often swallowed up by the endless to-do list—laundry that breeds like rabbits, dinners that don't cook themselves, errands that multiply overnight. Sometimes, by the time we even think about focusing on ourselves, there's barely anything left in the tank.

Here's the thing: time is going to pass anyway. What's important to recognize is that time isn't just passing by—it's making decisions for us when we don't make them ourselves. Every time we say "not yet" to our dreams, we're saying "yes" to the gap. Every time we choose comfort over courage, we're voting for the status quo.

I remember once thinking, *How hard can it be to have a baby and go back to work?*

Then I became a mother.

Sitting in that hospital room, holding my firstborn, I realized just how fast twelve weeks would vanish. Days felt like minutes. Minutes felt like seconds. I wrestled with the questions we all ask: *Do I take more time? Can we survive on one paycheck? Do I really leave my baby with strangers who might see him more than I do?*

I was deep in the gap—that space where you know you're about to expand but you're terrified you won't stretch far enough. Where every choice feels like you're betraying some version of yourself.

I went back to work anyway. Not because it was easy. Not because I had it all figured out. But because deep down, I knew I was meant to hold both—motherhood and career— even when it felt impossible.

During my maternity leave, I read *Lean In* by Sheryl Sandberg, and it lit a fire in me. When I returned to work, I walked into the offices of my two executive VPs— both fathers to daughters—and asked if I could start a Women in Construction group, a space to talk about the real challenges: work-life integration, personal growth, supporting each other.

Not only did they say yes—they bought the book for everyone. That group still exists today, now on a national level twelve years later. Because I chose to stretch instead of shrink, it's impacted hundreds of women and men who now know they aren't alone.

That taught me something powerful: growth isn't about showing up perfectly. It's about showing up fully—messy, brave, and all in. The gap isn't asking you to have all the answers—it's asking you to take the first step anyway to figure it out.

Every single day offers what I call "choice points." The alarm goes off—snooze or rise? An opportunity arises—step up or step back? A tough conversation looms—engage or avoid? A dream nudges your heart—act or dismiss?

Each choice point is a chance to either step toward your potential or stay exactly where you are. This isn't meant to overwhelm you—it's meant to remind you that expansion doesn't require huge leaps. Like we talked about in the last chapter, it requires consistent small choices in the direction of growth.

So how do we begin to build that bridge across the gap? I want to offer you a practical exercise that has transformed my life and the lives of countless others.

There's a massive difference between "I can't do it yet" and "I'm working toward it," between "It's not the right time" and "I'm making time," between "Someday I will" and "Today I begin."

For the next 30 days, write down everything you would do if there were no boundaries—no time restrictions, no financial limitations, no fear of judgment. Don't think too hard about it, just write. Set a timer for three to five minutes every day and let the words flow.

At the end of those 30 days, review what you've written. Look for patterns, for themes that keep showing up. What appears day after day? That's where you'll find the juice—the essence of what truly matters to you.

For me, it was speaking. I had always loved being on stage, even back in high school when I played the lead mother in *Cheaper by the Dozen.* Somehow, that passion got buried under years of "shoulds" and expectations.

Decades later, I find myself right back where I started—on stage, sharing my message. Do I know exactly where this path leads? Do I have the next three to six years mapped out? Hell no. But I feel the alignment. I know this particular gap is closing.

The truth is, we're never truly ready. We're never fully prepared for the risks we take, the new roles we step into, or the challenges that come with expansion. But the ones who cross the bridge of their gaps—those are the ones who discover just how much they're actually capable of.

Also, don't mistake necessary preparation for procrastination. The gap isn't asking you to be reckless—it's asking you to be *ready enough.* Ready enough to take the first step, even if you can't see the whole staircase.

Stop waiting for perfect conditions. Stop waiting for more time, more money, more confidence, more clarity. The gap will always have reasons why "not yet" makes sense.

Start today. Start messy. Start scared. Start anyway.

Because the cost of staying in the gap isn't just missed opportunities—it's the quiet regret of wondering "what if?" years from now.

Your potential is too valuable to live in the gap forever. The time to start closing it isn't someday—it's today.

What's your next move?

AUDACITY IN ACTION CHALLENGE

Keep a "Choice Points Journal" for one week. At the end of each day, write down:

1. One moment where you chose comfort over growth,
2. How you felt in that moment, and
3. What you would do differently if you could replay that moment. This simple practice makes you aware of your choice points and builds your "expansion muscle" for future decisions.

Bonus Challenge: This week, identify your biggest gap and take one concrete step toward closing it. Remember, the step doesn't have to be big—it just has to be in the right direction.

SHARE YOUR JOURNEY

⏱ "Today I'm choosing growth over comfort. What gap are you ready to close? #AudaciousExpansion"

Chapter 4:

BOLD BLUEPRINT, NO APOLOGIES

The moment you share your goals, they stop being whispers and start becoming blueprints.

Picture this: steel-toed boots. Hard hat crushing my long, blonde ponytail. I was standing on what everyone called a landfill but what I knew would become a seven-story hotel.

I was twenty-two years old. I had a fresh engineering degree from Villanova. I had zero clue what I was walking into.

The project manager hands me blueprints like he's passing me the morning paper. "You're leading MEP systems." Then he just... walks away.

Cool. No pressure.

MEP—mechanical, electrical, and plumbing systems. Those tiny systems that keep buildings from, oh I don't know, BURNING DOWN or flooding. Systems I'd barely *touched* in textbooks were suddenly mine to master.

My office? A job trailer with *bars on the windows.* On top of a landfill. (Glamorous, right?)

My classroom? Seven acres of dirt, dust, and men who'd been swinging hammers since before I could walk.

Then it happened. Lunch break. I was just trying to figure out where the hell I fit in this concrete jungle when—WHAM. A catcall. Loud. Sharp. Designed to shrink me down to size.

I froze.

That split second stretched like taffy. I could keep walking. I could pretend I didn't hear it. I could play it safe, stay small, blend in...

Or I could turn around.

So I planted those steel-toed boots in that dirt, looked that man dead in the eye, and said: "Don't ever talk to me that way. We ALL deserve respect. I might not know everything you know about construction, but there are things I know that you don't. Let's make this equal. Let's learn from each other."

(Okay, maybe I wasn't quite that direct or eloquent in the moment, but I got the gist across.)

Silence.

Long enough to make my stomach flip.

But in that silence? Something shifted. I earned his respect—and even more importantly, I earned my own.

That day taught me construction, like life, isn't about who's been there longest. It's about building something together. Every voice matters. Every beam, every wire, every human playing their part in creating something greater.

We rise together, or we don't rise at all.

WHEN SIDEWAYS IS THE NEW UP

But here's the thing about rising, I spent years thinking it was all about the title. Climb the ladder. Get the corner office. Check the boxes.

But the farther I climbed, the clearer it became that sometimes the biggest leaps in growth look like... sidesteps.

I'll never forget sitting in my boss's office, practically vibrating with ambition: "How do I grow more? Do more? BE more?"

His answer? "Get into operations. Learn the foundation. It might feel like a sidestep now, but it'll fast-track everything later."

He was right. And that taught me something crucial about blueprints: sometimes the most important expansions happen horizontally, not vertically.

In construction, we don't just build up. We reinforce laterally. We strengthen foundations by expanding them outward. We create support beams that run horizontally to hold up the entire structure. The most stable buildings aren't just tall—they're well-supported across every level.

I see this in relationships too. Some of my strongest connections started as lateral moves—the neighbor who became a lifelong friend, the acquaintance who became my accountability partner. Not climbing some social ladder, but expanding my foundation of support.

Your life blueprint works the same way. Sometimes expansion means climbing higher. Sometimes it means reaching wider. Sometimes it means digging deeper into what you already have. The beauty of a blueprint isn't its rigidity—it's its ability to accommodate growth in all directions.

But here's where many of us get stuck: we draft the blueprint, then forget to actually build from it. We get comfortable in the planning phase and never break ground. We stop asking "Am I really constructing the life I designed?" and start shuffling through the same set of plans like zombies on autopilot.

What I realized is that if I wanted to construct anything with intention, I had to stop endlessly revising and start building. I needed to get my hands dirty with actual construction.

And for me, that started with a pen.

Get this: you're 43% more likely to make a goal happen if you write it down. Forty-three percent. That's basically half the battle. And when you tell someone else about that goal? It jumps to 78%. (Which is wild, considering most of us would rather post a picture of our salad than admit what we actually want from life.)

So maybe you don't know every detail of your final structure. Maybe you're working with a limited budget and basic materials. Maybe you feel like you're staring at a blank drafting table trying to remember what you wanted to build.

You don't need the complete architectural plans—you just need a foundation sketch. A structural outline. A blueprint that says, "This is what I'm building."

So... when's the last time you did that?

When's the last time you sketched out a dream, not because it was practical or affordable or code-compliant—but because your soul whispered, "This matters"?

A confused architect builds nothing. And you, my friend, were not made to sit at the drafting table forever. You were made to build.

I was walking through my neighborhood golf course recently with earbuds in, and suddenly I stopped dead in my tracks.

Rachel Hollis was talking on the podcast I was listening to, and she said something that slapped me straight across the face (in the best way):

"Stop apologizing for who you are and what you want."

Oof. YES. That's it.

Listen: You can be grateful—*deeply* grateful—for the life you've built so far and still crave more. That's not greed. That's *growth*. That's *aliveness*. That's the holy discontent that calls us to expand, evolve, and level up.

I learned that firsthand when I made one of the boldest moves of my life. I was in my early twenties, living in suburbia, and after a breakup I decided to take a quantum leap to move into a city where I knew very few people—

Hoboken, New Jersey, right across the river from New York City.

I knew it would be scary. I didn't know exactly how I was going to do it, where I was going to live, how it was all going to happen, but I knew I needed a change. I needed something that was going to catapult me forward.

Those six months were probably the toughest—moving out of my comfortable place into a tiny apartment with two women I'd met online (which felt crazy at the time). My bedroom was literally big enough to fit a double bed and one small dresser. My rent doubled. My commute got much longer. But I knew I needed to expand. I needed to be around new people, in a new situation. I needed to dare myself and prove I could do it.

It was a really tough period, but I believe it was the springboard for everything else. It prepared me for the next change, giving me the ingredients so that when future challenges came, I was already used to adapting. They say the first cut is the deepest, but once you start, you realize it's going to heal—and you can do it again.

The blueprint wasn't mapped out perfectly, but I recognized it opened doors. Within a year of moving there, I bought my first place at age 22—a two-bedroom, super small brownstone walk-up with no central AC. I knew real estate was worth investing in, and it was probably one of the scariest yet best decisions I ever made. I couldn't afford it unless I had a roommate in that second bedroom (which was literally the size of a closet).

Looking back now, I'm proud of myself for being willing to take that risk. Over two decades later, I still own that property. That's where I truly laid the foundation and first bricks for growth, change, and calculated risks at an early age.

I still try to do that—calculated risks, not hazardous ones, but risks that push me into scary uncharted waters while always bringing me back to the blueprint I need. Every leap lays another brick in your blueprint.

Building a life you're proud of isn't just about career moves or real estate investments. It's about constructing experiences that matter. One tradition Andy and I have architected as a family is our annual summer adventure. Not a resort vacation—an adventure. Someplace new. Something unknown. Every summer, we pack up and go explore.

I always say there are four things I want to give my kids: love, faith, education, and experiences. Not the sit-in-a-pew-and-don't-move kind of faith—but that deep knowing that they're part of something bigger, that there's magic and purpose woven into their story. And even when the budget is tight, we find a way to give them that sense of wonder through travel. Every year somehow, someway, Andy and I manage to figure it out, make a spreadsheet, plan together and dream bigger than we ever thought imaginable.

This tradition started when the kids were just two and five, on a 14-day trip from Switzerland to Venice. I'll never forget those Alpine roads—winding paths, mountain peaks towering, kids dozing off in the backseat, and Andy holding my hand. We didn't know exactly where we were building each memory, and that was the point. It wasn't about fine dining (with toddlers? ha!) or five-star hotels. It was about being together in awe.

And every time I think, "We can't take the time," or "It's not in the budget," I flash back to moments like jumping off a cliff in Croatia, my kids watching from the shore. Or the year we road-tripped from San Francisco to Yosemite, up through Tahoe. We had a loose framework—1,300 miles— but no set plan for every day. One sweltering afternoon, I Googled "things to do nearby" and landed us on a last-minute rafting trip down the American River. Just us, a raft, some snacks, and nonstop laughter. One of our favorite memories to this day.

Each year, I laminate a map for the kids (yes, Type A forever) so they can track our journey. These trips have become a sacred part of our family's story.

Those are the moments that shape us as a family. The ones they'll never forget—and honestly, neither will I.

These moments remind me that the blueprint doesn't have to be flawless to be powerful. And yet, admittedly, I struggle here still constantly, thinking everything needs to be planned. That's where the "yang" of Andy reminds me (sometimes without saying a word) that it will all work out. We may not have the biggest house or the fanciest cars, but we've built a life rich with curiosity and connection.

Just like the blueprints I've used in the field, they're never perfect. Many times, what's on the drawing isn't what we build. There are mistakes. Revisions. But that sketch gives us direction. It keeps us building.

So—what's your construction status right now? Are you stuck in the planning phase? Building without direction? Working with blueprints that no longer serve you?

You don't need to have it all figured out. But you do need to start designing your unique blueprint.

Every quarter, I check in with myself: What have I built? What am I constructing? Do I need new plans? Updated permits? A whole new foundation?

That check-in helps me course-correct (and I remind you that it's not always easy to do). It helps me come back to my vision, my values, my voice.

Because life will life. The clock keeps ticking. What will we build with the time we have?

So start sketching. Start dreaming.

And then? Start building.

Your blueprint is uniquely designed to fit *you*. And unlike those construction plans that sit in drawers for months, this one gets better every time you act on it.

Anyone can imagine a beautiful structure, but architects and builders know that translating vision into reality requires detailed plans and precise execution.

Your life is the most important structure you'll ever build. Don't let it be constructed by chance or someone else's design.

Create your blueprint, expect some revisions along the way, and build something magnificent.

What will your masterpiece look like?

AUDACITY IN ACTION CHALLENGE

This week, create your unique blueprint. Not just a to-do list, but a vision of the life you want to build based on the uniqueness that defines who you are. Then identify one bold action that scares you a little but excites you a lot in building your vision. Take that first step—make the call, book the trip, have the conversation, or submit the application.

SHARE YOUR JOURNEY

✸ "I'm creating my unique blueprint and taking one audacious step toward it this week. What's your first bold move? #AudaciousExpansion"

Chapter 5

TRUE NORTH OR BUST

*Your limitations are not your destiny unless
you decide they are.*

Since my assault, I've handed each of my kids a gift. No, not
an envelope stuffed with cash or the latest gadget they were
secretly hoping for.

A compass.

Yep, a literal compass. Not flashy. Not what they expected.
But something that, I believe, will outlast anything shiny or
new. A reminder that life will try to throw you off course. You
will get lost. You will feel stuck. You'll get knocked down—
sometimes literally. But if you know your true north—your
deeper why—you'll find the strength to get back up and keep
moving forward. And faith that God will always lead you to
where you need to go.

They may not fully get the meaning yet, and that's okay. I plant the seeds anyway. I tell them: life will knock you down. The bills will pile up. People will leave. You'll get the diagnosis you weren't ready for. You'll lose the job, the dream, the security. But every time you get back up, every time you check that compass and take another step forward, you're building something unbreakable inside you.

This compass may be a cute metaphor, but it's also a lifeline. It's the gift that says: You're going to face storms. You're going to question everything. But when you know your why—when you understand the reason you're here—those storms can't sink you. They just reroute you.

BUILDING YOUR INNER COMPASS

I think about Apple's famous "Think Different"[1] campaign, which captured something powerful about the people who change the world:

"Here's to the crazy ones. The misfits. The rebels. The troublemakers. The round pegs in the square holes. The ones who see things differently. They're not fond of rules. And they have no respect for the status quo. You can quote them, disagree with them, glorify or vilify them. About the only thing you can't do is ignore them. Because they change things. They push the human race forward. And while some may see them as the crazy ones, we see genius. Because the people who are crazy enough to think they can change the world, are the ones who do."

But here's the part no one talks about—the courage, the grit, and the audacity it takes to keep going when the world tells you no. The people who change the world aren't just dreamers. They are the ones who get knocked down and refuse to stay down. When they feel lost, they consult their compass to find their true north again—their deeper purpose that drives them forward.

They have self-worth: knowing you belong in the room, even when others doubt you. They have resilience: the ability to push through setbacks, criticism, and rejection. They have authenticity: staying true to yourself, even when it's easier to conform.

Because the people who are audacious enough to believe in themselves—who refuse to back down—are the ones who rise. And resilience isn't just about enduring what life throws at you. It's about recognizing that you have the power to reshape what comes next.

And here's what Steve Jobs understood that most people miss: *"Everything around you that you call life was made up by people who are no smarter than you. And you can change it. You can influence it. You can build your own things that other people can use. Once you learn that, you'll never be the same."*[2]

That's the thing about true resilience—it isn't passive endurance. It's not just about weathering storms or finding shelter when life gets hard. It's about realizing that you have the power to build the shelter, chart a new course, and even change the forecast. The world isn't set in stone; it's shaped by those who refuse to accept "this is just how things are."

Your struggles aren't barriers; they're raw materials for building something better. Every setback becomes feedback. Every rejection becomes redirection. Every "no" becomes information you can use to create a different path forward.

My son Drew reminded me that the secret sauce to staying aligned with resilience really is consistency. It's showing up on the days when you want to throw in the towel, when it seems impossible, and when no one else is looking.

When Drew was just eight years old, he came to us with an idea that seemed ambitious for his age—he wanted to start his own business. While part of me thought he might be reaching too far, another part—the part that believes in audacity—was secretly thrilled.

Drew created a business called "Hole in One," where he would venture out onto our local golf course during the off-season winter months to collect lost golf balls. Before long, our garage was overflowing with hundreds, if not thousands, of golf balls.

By the time he turned ten, Drew had turned those collected golf balls into a $6,000 business. He would wake up early, load his wagon with cleaned and sorted golf balls, and sell them to golfers arriving for their morning rounds. He created value where others saw discarded items; he turned inconvenience into opportunity.

What made this remarkable wasn't just the business idea—it was his consistency. Some days, he'd return home empty-handed. Other days, he'd come back with nearly $100 in earnings. The results varied, but his commitment didn't waver. His compass remained focused on his true north—his purpose—regardless of daily outcomes.

Thomas Edison said, "I've not failed. I've just found 1,000 different ways that didn't work."

Drew embodied this philosophy without even knowing it. He taught me that success rarely hinges on having the highest IQ or the most resources—it's built on consistently showing up and having a reliable compass to navigate through the ups and downs.

Watching him with that consistency of being willing to do the hard work day after day reminded me that I needed to bring that same energy to my own pursuits. His example challenged me to be audacious, to be brave, and to stop playing it safe.

So what exactly makes up your expansion compass? How do you identify yours and learn to trust it? Through my journey, I've discovered three essential elements that form the foundation of this internal guidance system:

Values Alignment - Think of this as the "magnetic north" of your compass. When your actions align with your deeply held values, you never have to wonder if you're on the right path. You can feel it in your bones. Many of us move through life without clearly articulating what matters most to us. We absorb values from our families, cultures, and surroundings without questioning whether they truly resonate with who we are at our core.

It's not enough to simply know what you want —you also need to understand *why* you want it. The blueprint exercise from the previous chapter should have helped you identify your goals. But to keep your compass pointing true north, you must dig deeper to uncover the underlying values driving those aspirations. Knowing the "why" behind the wants for your life enables you to stay motivated and on track, even when the path gets difficult.

For example, if one of your goals is to get a promotion at work, reflect on why that matters to you. Is it because you value personal growth and relish new challenges? Or perhaps providing financial stability for your loved ones is a key priority. When your goals are anchored to your core values, you'll find greater clarity and resilience in pursuing them.

I recommend doing a values check-in at least quarterly. Ask yourself: Are my daily actions, my relationships, my work, and my goals aligned with what I truly value? If not, it's time to recalibrate.

Failure Analysis - Your compass requires regular calibration through honest assessment of what's working and what isn't. This is about growth, not beating yourself up.

Every time you stumble and then analyze that experience with compassion and curiosity, you're recalibrating your compass to be more accurate. Ask yourself: What worked, even if the overall outcome wasn't what I wanted? What specific actions led to this result? What will I do differently next time?

The most determined people I know don't avoid failure—they embrace it as essential feedback for their journey.

Expansion Rituals - These are the consistent practices that keep you focused on your true north. For me, it's my morning routine with exercise, journaling, and meditation. These rituals create space for you to check in with yourself, to listen to your inner wisdom, and to recommit to your path.

When life gets chaotic—and it will—these rituals become even more important. They're your anchor points, the practices that remind you who you are and what matters most.

Every day, you'll face those choice points—moments where you must choose which way to go. Some decisions will be small, like whether to have that difficult conversation or how to respond to criticism. Others will be monumental, like changing careers, ending relationships, or taking a stand on something that matters to you.

Your expansion compass—carefully calibrated through values alignment, failure analysis, and consistent rituals—will point you toward your true north. Sometimes, the needle will waver. Sometimes, external forces will try to pull it off course. That's when you need your compass most.

Before we turn the page into Part Two and talk about breaking boundaries wide open, we have to know where you're headed. We can't unlock the next level of this journey until you pause here. Reflect. Reconnect with your why.

This is your map check. Your refuel station. ***Don't skip it.***

Because in Part Two, we're about to push boundaries on that map and venture into brand new territory.

Buckle up. Let's go.

AUDACITY IN ACTION CHALLENGE

This week, recalibrate your compass.

First, identify the three most important values that form your magnetic north. Write them down somewhere you'll see them daily.

Second, establish one simple ritual that will help you maintain your compass—whether it's five minutes of morning reflection or a weekly values check-in. Commit to it for the next month.

SHARE YOUR JOURNEY

✺ "I'm recalibrating my expansion compass and identifying my true north. What values guide your compass? #AudaciousExpansion"

Part 2:

BREAKING YOUR BOUNDARIES

Don't forget to download your free journal before continuing.

Chapter 6:

SMASH THE AUTOPILOT

*Life isn't a race; it's a journey where everyone
operates in their own time zone.*

It was 4:45 AM, and I found myself already dreading the day
ahead. From the outside, my life looked perfect: a great job, a
loving marriage, a happy family with a one- and three-year-
old, and all the external markers of success. Yet there I sat
in my car in the parking lot, feeling empty, wondering how
many more mornings I would spend this way.

The questions rolling through my mind were relentless:
*Where was my path? Where was my purpose? Where was my
passion? Had I lost my light? Was it gone forever? Would that
flame ever reignite? Or was I destined to live this way—going
through the motions, working for the next forty years to support
someone else's dreams?*

That morning, I realized we operate on autopilot more often than we realize. We cruise through life at a steady, comfortable speed because autopilot conserves our energy. It's the easiest way to navigate our days—we don't have to press the accelerator or think about our destination. Autopilot can feel easy and comfortable, until one day we wake up feeling deeply discontent, wondering how we got so far off course. In the process of living on autopilot, we lost track of being intentional about our lives and choices.

Many of us live this way: rising to the same alarm, eating the same breakfast, following the same routines. While I believe in the power of habits and consistency, sometimes we must disengage autopilot to truly expand our lives.

This tendency to follow expected paths isn't something that develops in adulthood—for many of us, it's been conditioned since our earliest experiences in life.

THE SMALL FISHBOWL

There's a principle I've come to understand through both observation and experience that explains why some people soar while others stay stagnant. Consider anyone you admire—anyone who has pushed boundaries, transcended limitations, or achieved something greater than themselves. If we interviewed them, the majority would say, "I decided to take the leap." In other words, I decided to leave the small fishbowl and jump into the vast ocean.

What do I mean by this? Place a fish in a tiny tank and it shrinks its potential to fit. Move it to open water, and suddenly it grows into what it was always meant to be.

So, what size tank are you currently living in? Are you choosing environments that force you to shrink, or ones that invite you to expand? Are you keeping your life on cruise control, operating on autopilot in familiar but limiting spaces? Or are you deliberately seeking the open waters—new heights, unexplored territories that challenge you to grow into your full potential?

For me, the answer became clear when I looked back at my own pattern of choices. Even before I understood what I was doing, I had been unconsciously choosing the bigger tank every time. My journey toward breaking free from society's predetermined paths began long before I realized what I was doing.

After my freshman year of college, I spent a summer working on Nantucket Island with some friends. When we arrived, I watched my girlfriends automatically gravitate towards the traditional cashier positions. "That's the easy job and we get out early," they insisted, following the path of least resistance.

Something inside me rebelled against that notion. When the manager mentioned an opening in the dairy department, I immediately volunteered. His eyes narrowed skeptically. "Are you sure you want this position? This is manual labor. Most people in that department are men."

His doubt only strengthened my resolve. "Challenge accepted."

That summer, while my friends scanned groceries in air-conditioned comfort, I dragged heavy U-boats—flat carts loaded with milk gallons—across the store. This was an old-school grocery store—probably something from the 1950s—where everything had to be manually loaded. Literally. I had to load all the refrigerators and work in the freezer. In fact, they ended up giving me an insulated vest so I would stay warm. They also nicknamed me Dairy Queen.

The work was physically demanding and left me with yes, impressive arm definition, but also something far more valuable: the satisfaction of choosing the road less traveled.

This pattern continued throughout my life. When engineering led to construction opportunities, I heard that same doubtful voice: "I didn't go to school for construction." But the spirit that led me to the dairy department whispered back, "Might as well try it." That decision opened doors I never knew existed.

But let's be real—even those types of leaps can become stagnant after a while. Success in one area doesn't make you immune to falling into comfortable routines. Which led me to sitting in that parking lot at 3:45 AM. I knew there was something more I could stretch myself to, but I couldn't see what it was yet.

However, I was about to make a decision that would change my life. My entrepreneurial spirit decided to explore network marketing.

Now, before you roll your eyes and think "Oh great, here comes the pyramid scheme pitch"—hear me out.

Many people judged my decision. Many thought I was making a mistake. Honestly, I questioned it myself, thinking, "This isn't for me. This is for people looking to earn extra spending money."

But I truly believe that network marketing was the exact type of alignment I didn't even know I was looking for. I'd always been into health and wellness—teaching fitness classes for almost 15 years, owning my own gym, using running as my therapy for years. The older I got, I realized nutrition was *everything* to me. After suffering with my eating disorder for so many years, I recognized that fueling my body with the right things to be able to show up as the best version of myself was absolutely critical.

And it was these products that I put in my body that lit me up like a Christmas tree. They allowed me to feel better, to share with my husband (who ended up losing 22 pounds), with my best friend (who finally started sleeping through the night), and with friends who were able to take their nutrition to the next level.

Consider for a moment, how many things do you love and share every day? A good plumber, amazing boots, your favorite jeans—and you don't get paid a dime for those recommendations, right?

Well, here I was being compensated for sharing products that I *actually* loved, products that would light up other people, products that I would give to myself and my own kids (and still take religiously, by the way.).

I dared to say yes to an opportunity that excited me. I was choosing a bigger pond, even though I had no idea how to swim in it yet. But it aligned with my values so my compass knew it was the right way to go, and I trusted that.

As a result, this was an opportunity that showed me I could build something, that I could multiply, that I could create a stream of income that would change my family's life. But the best part? It was the community—a community of other light-bringers, a community of people who lit me up, a community that showed me what was possible, that believed in me and would literally stand on chairs for me.

I worked intensely for three years to grow that business into an international team of over 25,000 people. The goal was to show people they could dream bigger and unlock their potential.

I'll never forget a woman named Carrie that I met through what seemed like chance but felt like divine alignment. She had three sons and, unbeknownst to me initially, a for-sale sign on her front lawn.

During our conversation, she shared that her husband was unemployed while she worked as a teacher, struggling to make ends meet. The for-sale sign represented their last resort—rising property taxes had made their family home, where they had raised their three sons, financially impossible.

I presented the opportunity to join my team, to link arms with passionate, like-minded people committed to expansion. Today, that same woman reminds me that because she said yes, because she dared to join us, that for-sale sign came down. She still lives in that house.

That's what happens when you turn off autopilot and start making conscious choices about your direction. She chose to leave her small fishbowl and jump into the ocean. And it changed everything for her like it did for me.

Listen, I'd be lying if I said this journey was without struggle. Breaking free from autopilot has been difficult for me at times because, frankly, I appreciate autopilot too. It feels easy, safe, and comfortable—and I do LOVE routines (and checklists). There have been countless moments when I've wanted to decline opportunities, to say "not right now" because the stretch felt uncomfortable.

Recently, my now twelve-year-old son Drew was accepted into a young entrepreneurship program for high schoolers. I knew he would be the youngest participant and that the program would be challenging for both of us.

I actually called the director. "Do you really think this is appropriate? I'm concerned he'll struggle or fall behind."

Then I reconsidered: Would I keep him in the small fishbowl? Is this the legacy I want to leave—choosing safety over growth?

He had earned acceptance, so why would I limit his potential? Yes, it would require more effort from me. Yes, he might experience stress, but isn't that what real-world preparation entails?

After one particularly challenging three-hour session, I could see Drew's frustration during our drive home. For the first time, I witnessed my talkative son experience genuine stress and process it largely in silence.

I recognized he was being pushed, processing, and determining how to navigate these new challenges. The earlier we experience difficulties, the better we develop resilience. He was growing to meet his new environment.

After allowing time for reflection, we had a meaningful conversation. I reminded him that he was raising his standards. Being in a room with older children for such an incredible opportunity was making him stronger, sharper, and more capable.

Expansion is a process. In a world promising instant results and overnight success, we've forgotten that valuable transformations require time, patience, and yes, discomfort. It means getting out of autopilot and challenging ourselves.

So how do we actually do it? How do we stop operating on autopilot and start making conscious choices about growth on our path?

Here are a few ideas that you just may want to try (and remember, not all will apply, but if we don't put these things into action, then how can we truly expand?):

- **Create Pattern Interrupts:** Small routine changes that force you out of autopilot. Take different routes to work. Use your non-dominant hand for simple tasks. Try unfamiliar foods. These minor disruptions make your brain pay attention and create new neural pathways.
- **Schedule Expansion Time:** Block calendar time specifically for comfort zone expansion. Even thirty minutes weekly dedicated to new experiences can shift perspective and create momentum for larger changes.

- **Challenge Your "I Am" Statements:** Our identities often maintain autopilot. "I'm not a morning person." "I'm bad with money." "I'm not creative." Challenge these limiting beliefs by adding "yet" or reframing entirely.

- **Find Your Bigger Pond:** Sometimes you need to deliberately place yourself in environments where you're not the most experienced, knowledgeable, or successful person. Bigger ponds force growth in ways comfort never can.

- **Choose Your Co-Pilots:** Much depends on the five people we surround ourselves with. Who joins you on this journey? People who prefer autopilot and simplicity, or people who rev your engine, excite you, expand you, and elevate you to the next level?

Research shows that 85% of our success and happiness comes from well-developed relationships. Your willingness to break free from autopilot is influenced by the voices in your ear and the examples around you. Stop settling for passengers. Start choosing co-pilots.

Co-pilots are those who won't let you stay small. People who see your potential even when you can't. People who understand that comfort zones are cozy, but nothing ever grows there.

I get so fired up about this that I turned it into one of my favorite keynote speeches: *The Audacity to Make Meaningful Connections.* If you

MEANINGFUL CONNECTIONS

want a peek, scan the QR code for my favorite ways to make meaningful connections—I'd love for you to experience it.

Breaking free from autopilot isn't about constant chaos or rejecting all routine. It's about making conscious choices for expansion toward your biggest dreams—and recognizing what keeps you stagnant.

Your dreams are waiting. But they're not waiting forever.

So, I challenge you: dare yourself to step out of that small fishbowl, off that hamster wheel, away from that familiar road. Choose the bigger pond where true expansion awaits.

AUDACITY IN ACTION CHALLENGE

This week, intentionally break out of autopilot in two specific ways:

First, practice "Pattern Interrupt"—for three consecutive days, intentionally disrupt your usual patterns. Take a different route to work, use your non-dominant hand for simple tasks, or try a new food.

Second, put yourself in a "Bigger Pond"—a situation where you're not the most knowledgeable person in the room. Take a class above your skill level, join a group with people more successful than you, or have a conversation with someone whose achievements you admire.

SHARE YOUR JOURNEY

✺ "I'm taking my life off autopilot this week and already feeling more alive! What's one way you're breaking free from your routine? #AudaciousExpansion"

Chapter 7

ROOTED & RESILIENT AF

Before you can expand outward, you must strengthen within.

There are certain pieces of wisdom that get passed down to us in life. Some we rebel against, and others we never forget.

A piece of advice was shared with my sister Kim and me as little girls from my mom that I still remember to this day. I reference it frequently in my keynotes, and now I hear myself saying it to my own children.

"Life is like a triangle. First comes your health, then comes your family, and then comes your job, career, or entrepreneurial spirit."

The triangle is a simple but powerful concept that highlights the three essential pillars of a fulfilling life: health, relationships, and work. Each corner of the triangle represents a crucial aspect that, when properly nurtured and integrated, creates a solid foundation for personal growth and success.

The first corner is your health—your physical, mental, emotional, and spiritual well-being. This forms the basis of your ability to show up fully in all other areas of your life. Just as the airplane safety instructions advise putting on your own oxygen mask first, prioritizing your health enables you to be the best version of yourself for others.

The second corner represents your family and relationships—the people who bring love, support, and meaning to your life. While no relationship is perfect, fostering strong connections with your core people is essential to a sense of belonging and purpose.

The third corner is your work or career—how you contribute to the world and find fulfillment through your talents and passions.

What I've learned over the years is this wasn't teaching me sequential priority—first health, then family, then work. It was teaching me something far more important: integration. These three elements don't compete; they complement. When properly structured, they create a foundation that can support expansion in all areas of your life.

THE FOUNDATION PHASE

Integration isn't about perfect balance (because *balance is bullshit*). Sometimes the triangle will stand up perfectly, and other times it won't—and that's acceptable, because that reflects life itself. Sometimes one side receives more priority than the others, and that's normal because perfect balance is impossible.

Integration is about creating a structure where each element reinforces the others.

When your health is strong, you show up better for your family and work. When your family relationships are nourishing, you have the emotional support to pursue career ambitions. When your work is aligned with your purpose, it energizes rather than depletes you.

When I think about this triangle, I'm reminded of the early days of my construction career. I'd walk onto a site and watch as the foundation was laid—each element critical, each measurement precise. One small mistake in the foundation and the entire structure would be compromised.

It wasn't the flashy finishes that determined whether a building would stand for generations—it was the unseen, underground work that no one would ever admire or photograph.

Your life operates no differently. The most visible aspects—career achievements, public recognition, social media highlights—are just the finishes. What matters most is the foundation: your health, your relationships, your impact.

Just like the buildings I used to construct, it's brick by brick, mortar joint by mortar joint. This doesn't happen overnight. You don't simply wake up one day and figure this out. I believe everything is figure-out-able (and I believe we're given the strength and wisdom to figure it out), but it takes time, consistency, and active building (and sometimes rebuilding).

As the triangle grows larger—as each corner becomes stronger and more stable—you'll have more space in the middle to work on yourself, your goals, and your dreams. When you've built the foundation of your health, worked on your family relationships, and allocated passionate time to provide for your family, the center expands. In the middle, you have extra time to determine how you're going to grow, how you're going to expand, and how you're going to leave this earth as the best version of yourself.

The beauty of the triangle principle lies in its ability to create sustainability. When your expansion is built on a solid foundation of health, relationships, and purposeful work, it can withstand the inevitable challenges that arise. I've seen people achieve remarkable short-term success while neglecting their foundation. They rise quickly, shine brightly, and then collapse spectacularly. Their expansion wasn't sustainable because it wasn't supported by a structure that could endure.

I've watched too many people try to expand their lives without first ensuring their foundation is strong. They add new goals, new commitments, new aspirations onto a shaky base. It's like trying to add floors to a building with a cracked foundation—the higher you go, the more dangerous it becomes. Before you can expand outward, you must strengthen within. Before you can reach new heights, you must ensure your base can support the weight of your ambitions.

This is why a restructuring phase often feels like a step backward. You may need to pull back from certain commitments, simplify your schedule, or say no to opportunities that don't align with your triangle. You might need to invest time in healing your body, repairing relationships, or clarifying your career direction before you can safely expand.

In Chapter 2, I mentioned my eating disorder. Through most of my twenties, I was living proof of what happens when you ignore that first corner of the triangle. The eating disorder became my way of trying to control everything in my life when everything else felt chaotic. Instead of expanding, I was shrinking—literally and figuratively.

I remember coming back after my freshman year of college and catching a glimpse of myself in the mirror. My hair was so thin you could see my scalp. My teeth weren't in great shape. I looked... fragile. Breakable. Like a strong wind could knock me over.

For fifteen years, I chose the eating disorder over everything else. My foundation was crumbling. My relationships suffered because I was constantly distracted by food thoughts and rituals. My work suffered because I didn't have the mental clarity or physical energy to show up fully. I was trying to build a life on a foundation made of sand.

The restructuring I had to do wasn't glamorous. I had to pull back from social situations that triggered me. I had to say no to activities that centered around food. I had to simplify my life to create space for healing. It felt like I was moving backward while everyone else was moving forward.

Even today, I still have moments—small struggles here and there—that remind me this is a journey, not a destination. But what I've learned is that healing doesn't happen in isolation. It happens when you start building that triangle properly, with health as the non-negotiable first corner.

Don't mistake this necessary restructuring for failure or regression. Think of it as excavation before building a stronger structure—you have to dig deep before you can build high.

This requires periodic reassessment. Just as buildings need regular maintenance and sometimes structural reinforcement, your foundation needs ongoing attention. Ask yourself regularly:

- **Health Check:** How am I caring for my physical, mental, emotional, and spiritual well-being? Where am I compromising my health for other priorities, and how can I restructure to prioritize wellness?
- **Relationship Evaluation:** Are my closest relationships nurturing or draining? Am I investing time and energy in the people who matter most? Where do I need to repair, strengthen, or perhaps distance myself from relationships?
- **Work Alignment:** Does my work—whether a career, business, volunteer role, or creative pursuit—align with my strengths and purpose? Does it contribute to or detract from my overall life? What adjustments would create better alignment?

When your triangle is properly structured, it expands naturally. The stronger your foundation becomes, the more capacity you develop for growth in all areas. This creates an upward spiral where each element of your triangle strengthens the others. Your expansion isn't just in one dimension but multidimensional—you're becoming more of who you're meant to be in every aspect of your life.

You're no longer trying to force expansion against resistance. Instead, expansion becomes the natural result of a well-built foundation.

And as my mother wisely noted, within this expanding triangle is a growing space—the center where you can explore, dream, and pursue your unique purpose. The stronger your foundation, the more freedom you have to expand into that purpose.

Don't let your triangle become about surviving—it should be about thriving. It's about creating a life so solid, so well-built, that when storms come (and they will), you don't just weather them; you use them to grow even stronger.

That's what being rooted and resilient AF really means.

AUDACITY IN ACTION CHALLENGE

This week, conduct a foundation audit and take one concrete action to strengthen each corner of your triangle.

Health: Identify one health habit that would significantly improve your foundation (whether physical, mental, emotional, or spiritual) and commit to practicing it daily for one week. This might be meditation, movement, journaling, or anything that genuinely supports your wellbeing.

Relationships: Have one conversation you've been avoiding with someone important in your life. This might be expressing appreciation, setting a boundary, resolving a conflict, or simply reconnecting authentically.

Work: Identify one aspect of your work that feels misaligned with your values or strengths and take one step toward better alignment. This might involve delegating a task that drains you, having a conversation with your manager, or dedicating time to a project that lights you up.

SHARE YOUR JOURNEY

✺ "I'm restructuring my foundation using the Triangle Principle—health, relationships, work—to create sustainable expansion. Which corner of your triangle needs the most attention right now? #AudaciousExpansion"

Chapter 8:

DITCH BUSY. CHOOSE ABUNDANCE.

We're not busy—we're abundant.

Let's start with a mission that's close to my heart: helping you take the word "busy"—that crutch of a four-letter B word—completely out of your vocabulary. Because ditching "busy" isn't just about changing your language. It's about reclaiming your life from the tyranny of overwhelm and stepping into something much bigger—living abundantly, intentionally, and audaciously.

We're all moving at a pace that I don't know if our bodies were designed to handle. Most days, I have twenty-two tabs open in my mind. I said this to someone recently and they started laughing. "Tabs?" "Yes, like your computer, where you can barely find your last Google search because there's so much running."

But why? Because being busy has become a badge of honor, and I have worn it proudly for four decades. This past year, I decided to remove the word from my vocabulary. Not because I don't have a lot on my plate or because I'm not constantly trying to get one more load of laundry done, one more dish out of the dishwasher, or one more item off my checklist.

Instead, I decided to replace the word "busy" with "abundant." I must admit, at first this sounded a bit cocky, but give it a try. "I am abundant today" versus "I am busy. I'm so busy." How much better does it feel just changing that language? When I say I'm abundant, I'm reminded that my full plate is a blessing. I'm not overwhelmed; I'm overflowing. I'm not weighed down; I'm lifted up by the opportunities, relationships, and responsibilities in my life. This mindset shift doesn't erase the work—it reframes it.

THE POWER OF ABUNDANCE THINKING

This reframing represents the essence of moving from scarcity to abundance. The scarcity mindset tells us: "I don't have enough time." "I'm always behind." "Everyone else is doing more than me." "I'll never get it all done."

The abundance mindset reframes to: "I have the time I need for what truly matters." "I'm exactly where I need to be right now." "My journey is uniquely mine—comparison serves no purpose." "I can focus on what's important and put the other things on the back burner."

Abundance thinking changes how we experience our lives. And it's not just feel-good stuff. The research backs this up in some pretty incredible ways:

Enhanced Well-Being: Studies on optimistic thinking patterns show measurable benefits. Research by Scheier and Carver found that optimistic people demonstrate 23% better immune function and are 13% less likely to experience depression. When we reframe our full lives as abundant rather than overwhelming, we're literally rewiring our brains for better health outcomes.[1]

Improved Performance: Carol Dweck's research on growth mindset—a key component of abundance thinking—shows that people who believe in their capacity to grow perform 40% better academically and professionally than those with fixed mindsets. When you see your packed schedule as opportunities rather than burdens, you approach challenges with greater capability and resilience.[2,3]

Better Decision-Making: Research by Mani and colleagues reveals that scarcity mindset actually reduces cognitive capacity by 13-14 IQ points, while abundance thinking frees up mental resources for clearer decision-making. People operating from scarcity make 40% more errors in important choices compared to those with abundance mindsets.[4,5]

Stronger Social Connections: Positive psychology research shows that people who practice gratitude and abundance-focused thinking are 31% more likely to help others and build supportive relationships. When you're not constantly worried about not having enough time or energy, you're more generous with both.[6]

Pretty compelling case for ditching "busy," right?

When I say we all get the same 24 hours each day, that's the same 1,440 minutes, the same 86,400 seconds. No more, no less. Oprah gets 24 hours. Beyoncé gets 24 hours. Your neighbor who seems to have it all together? She gets 24 hours too.

So why do some people seem to create magic with their time while others feel like they're drowning in it?

I've depleted myself more times than I'd like to admit. I've literally been that woman on the bathroom floor, holding back tears before walking into a meeting, or while trying to show up for my child's play with a smile, while knowing my energy was gone. How much can I pack into my week? How many things can I check off my list? I was holding my energy expenditure as a trophy but it was draining me.

The older I get, the more I realize I need to protect that energy. The more I realize I need to stop wearing that faux badge of achievement.

I'll never forget about ten years ago, going to a conference where we took this personality test about energy drain. One of the instructors came up to me afterward and said, "I've never seen anyone with such a massive energy drain."

I looked at him like he was crazy. Me? I was the Energizer Bunny (yes, I even dressed up as that a few years ago for an adult Halloween party and my husband was the battery; I won the contest that year)—I'd keep going until you unplugged me or took the battery out. That's how I lived most of my days. Up early, and when my head finally hits that pillow, I sleep like a baby.

What that instructor meant was that I was constantly giving so much with everything I did that I was draining myself.

When he pointed out my energy drain, he didn't look at me with admiration. He looked at me and said, "You need to change something." From that day forward, I made a conscious choice to become more intentional of fueling my own energy—mental, physical, emotional, spiritual, all of my energy meters.

How are you adding to your energy bank account every day? We only get so much energy every day. Who's getting it? Where are you investing it? Are these the right places?

I've observed many people, including myself, pour energy into individuals who don't necessarily want or deserve it. Several years ago, I realized I needed to protect my energy and decide how much to invest in people who wouldn't reciprocate.

This recognition transformed my relationships. I had been trying extensively with certain important people who simply weren't showing up as I hoped. Initially, I felt angry and disappointed that they weren't meeting my expectations.

Then I realized I was creating expectations they weren't willing to meet. I faced a choice: continue pouring negative energy onto negative energy, or surround myself with people who elevated my energy and made me feel capable of extraordinary things?

There's someone particularly close to me—a family member who once played a meaningful role in my life. She distanced herself significantly, creating an eight-year source of pain. When this first happened, I took it personally. I kept thinking it was me. The more I reflected on that situation, I realized it was never actually about me anyway. For many of these situations that we face like that one, it's not usually about us at all. It's about that person and what they're wrestling with.

After investing tremendous energy, tears, sleepless nights, and therapy sessions, I reached this conclusion: it's acceptable to step away. I recently read Mel Robbins' book *LET THEM*, and it reminded me of this truth. But it was the "LET ME" part that hit hardest—I was the only one I could change, not my family member.[7]

When we start to remember that it's not about us, we can walk into audacious expansion because we're not wasting our energy where it doesn't serve us. When we pour energy into appropriate vessels, our energy multiplies. When we pour it where it doesn't belong, our energy diminishes.

The same goes for the things we choose to do and how we spend our time.

Someone once said to me, "*No* can be a complete sentence." *NO.* The more I say no to things that don't serve me, the more energy and time I find to do the things that do serve me. For so many years I wanted to be everything to everybody, and realized many years later I was serving no one in this situation.

Never forget that your energy is a precious resource. By being intentional about where you direct it, you create space for what truly matters. This is the essence of living authentically and in alignment with your values.

As you learn to say no to what doesn't serve you and yes to what does, you'll find that abundance flows naturally into your life. Abundance through the richness of experiences, relationships, and personal growth.

LIVING ABUNDANTLY EVERY DAY

Delivering a TEDx talk was such a significant goal of mine. I remember manifesting it clearly—believing it would happen—and it did. Family and friends showed up, I received accolades, and we capped it off with a celebration dinner. On paper, it was everything I had dreamed of.

Yet even in the middle of all that joy, I don't think I ever truly applauded myself. I never paused to acknowledge: *I fulfilled a dream. And I did an excellent job.*

I can still see it: walking out to the car with a huge bouquet from my husband in one hand, holding his hand with the other. He had just congratulated and honored me, and then he looked at me seriously and asked, "What's next?"

Now, he didn't say it because he thought I needed to do more. He said it because he knows me so well. He knows how my brain works—always scanning the horizon for the next challenge. But in that moment, it landed like a gut punch.

The TEDx had been over for less than an hour, the adrenaline still pulsing through me, and already he knew my mind was moving on to the "more."

What he couldn't have known was how powerful that question would become for me. Even now, it stops me in my tracks.

How many experiences like this do *we* all have? We pour ourselves into a goal, finally accomplish it, and then skip right past the celebration. We don't pause to recognize how far we've come. Instead, we slip back into the loop of, *What's next? What's unfinished? What didn't I get done on the list?*

And all that does is keep us spinning on the wheel—constantly depleted, constantly unaccomplished, constantly frustrated that we haven't done enough or *been* enough. That keeps us stuck in that busy mindset and we miss out on the abundance.

This is why I love keeping what I call an "Audacious Badass List"—a record of things I've accomplished. These are things I've worked really hard for, things I've forgotten to stop and congratulate myself for. Occasionally when I'm feeling depleted or behind, usually because I'm playing the comparison game with someone else, I take that list out. I say, "Damn. This is my list, my goals, and the things I've already achieved and conquered."

Stop and relish them. For me, that means taking the moment to remember what I felt like when I stepped onto that TEDx stage, when I crossed the finish line of the Chicago marathon, when I experienced the birth of my two most precious children. What are the things you have accomplished?

I want you to start building your own "Audacious Badass List" right now. (I encourage you to make it in the notes of your phone so you have it with you at all times). Capture every victory, every breakthrough, every moment you've been audacious. Every time you think of something while journaling from this point forward, add it to your list. Save it. Scan it. Reference it whenever you need a reminder of just how incredible you are.

But celebration is just one piece of living abundantly. The real magic happens when you start structuring your days to reflect abundance rather than scarcity.

As I've tried to figure out how to live more abundantly, I've realized that time blocking has been one of the best strategies for me. When I was writing this book, working on a podcast, and memorizing a keynote, I decided: "I'm going to take an hour out of my day, and I am going to work on this. I'm going to work on me."

Instead of trying to tackle everything simultaneously, I block it. I find time on most weekends to examine my calendar, decide what needs to be added—and quite frankly, what really needs to be removed. Because I'm one person with one battery. How much do I want to give each day, and what do I want to give it to?

Time blocking is the simplest way to manage time and priorities. Did you know that we are actually horrible multi-taskers? Research shows that when we have one task interrupted, our brains take an average of 23 minutes and 15 seconds to return to the original task.[8] Science tells us that multitasking is mostly a myth. Only about 2% of people can multitask effectively.[9] The other 98% of us? We're just really good at fooling ourselves.

So let's get real about time blocking. Identify what you need to work on for the day. Determine when you're the most productive. Schedule your time blocks.

I love color-coding my time blocks—each area of my life getting a specific color. If there is too much of one color, I reevaluate my schedule. Be sure to block off personal time as well and defend that time like it's any other important meeting on your calendar. Because guess what? That time with yourself IS the most important meeting of your day.

This structure doesn't limit your freedom—it creates it. Jocko Willink nailed this in his book *Discipline Equals Freedom* when he wrote that discipline is the pathway to liberation.[10] (And if a Navy SEAL says discipline creates freedom, I'm listening.) When you're intentional about your time, you naturally start making abundant choices. You begin each day with gratitude instead of panic. You replace "I have to" with "I get to." You create rituals to acknowledge achievements rather than rushing to the next goal. You curate your environment to inspire rather than drain you.

Keep in mind that these aren't all separate practices; they're all part of the same abundance mindset that can equally acknowledge how amazing everything is while also keeping you open for "more" when the time and season says it's go time.

Life won't slow down, but the mindset in which you approach it will help you feel like you haven't lost control of the passing time.

So many people wait for the "perfect time" for things to feel easier or for readiness to miraculously appear. But research shows that 72% of workers not in their dream job regret it, and 61% would trade what they're doing now to pursue that childhood dream[11]. And when researchers dug into the deepest, most enduring regrets, they found it's not failed action that haunts people—but the dreams they never chased[12].

Moving from scarcity to abundance is ultimately a choice you make moment by moment, day by day. It's a practice of noticing when you've slipped into scarcity thinking and gently guiding yourself back to abundance. It's recognizing that even amid difficulties, there is enough—enough time, enough resources, enough capacity within you to meet what life brings.

The shift from "busy" to "abundant" may seem like a small change in vocabulary, but it represents a profound transformation in how we experience our days. When we stop wearing busyness as a badge of honor and start recognizing the abundance in our lives, we create space for what truly matters.

Your energy is your most precious currency. Spend it wisely. Protect it fiercely. Invest it in people and pursuits that multiply it back to you.

Because when you're abundant—truly abundant—you don't just change your own life. You become a permission slip for everyone around you to live abundantly too.

AUDACITY IN ACTION CHALLENGE

This week, undertake a three-part Abundance Reset:

Part 1: For one full week, eliminate the word "busy" from your vocabulary. Replace it with "abundant" or another term that reflects fullness rather than depletion.

Part 2: Start building your Audacious Badass List. Identify at least five achievements, moments of courage, or times you've been audacious that you've never properly celebrated.

Part 3: Track your energy levels for three days. Note what activities, people, and environments drain you versus energize you. Make one concrete change to protect your energy based on your findings.

SHARE YOUR JOURNEY

✸ "I'm shifting from a scarcity mindset to an abundance mindset by dropping the 'busy' badge and celebrating my achievements. What helps you recognize the abundance in your life? #AudaciousExpansion"

Chapter 9

CRUSH THE CAGES;
OPEN YOUR CIRCLE

*Our limitations aren't really about the circumstances
we face — they're about the stories we tell ourselves
about those circumstances.*

We all carry invisible baggage. Stories whispered in childhood. Messages absorbed before we even knew we were listening. Beliefs about ourselves that took root so early, so quietly, that we've forgotten they're not facts— they're just stories.

As a parent for over a decade at this point, I recognize that when someone once said parenting is the most rewarding and the hardest role, they were onto something. Such truth. It is not easy, and let me tell you, I have made plenty of wrong turns raising Drew and Adelyn. I am far from perfect, but the one thing I do know, just like other parents out there, including my own, is that we always try our best.

My childhood was no different. I was raised by my mom, a school teacher, and my dad, a businessman. I had a little sister who has since become an incredible parent to two amazing kids.

I inherited both gifts and limitations from my upbringing. A love of learning and adventure. A strong work ethic. But also a belief that I had to earn love through performance, that my value was tied to external validation, and that emotional needs were inconvenient at best.

I grew up in a household where love was complicated at times. Where achievement was celebrated but emotional connection felt fragile. I watched my father, so devoted to work that many weeks he left before I woke up, and I didn't see him until bedtime. My mom poured her heart and soul into teaching in our school system, constantly praised for her devotion to education. My sister was a star athlete who became my favorite playmate.

What I absorbed from watching these dynamics was that worth came through accomplishment—my value measured by how little space I took up, my lovability determined by how much I could achieve.

Like many families, mine was a mixture of deep love and deep wounds. Parents who tried their best with the tools they had, but who carried their own limitations, their own struggles, their own stories of not being enough. I watched patterns of workaholism, perfectionism, and emotional distance play out in ways that shaped my understanding of relationships, success, and self-worth.

This book isn't about dissecting my childhood, but rather acknowledging that we all have experiences that have shaped us, hurt us, and ultimately helped us grow. Mine was no different. I share this not to assign blame, which never gets us anywhere, but to remind us that we're not alone, and what we see on the surface isn't always the full story.

We are taught by those we watch but also in living out our own experiences. For example, marriage has taught me that it's not easy, but it can be transformative. Andy and I have been together for over a decade, and while I feel incredibly blessed to have married someone who encourages me and supports my dreams, we're far from perfect. There are days when we don't see eye to eye, days when I feel like we're two ships passing in the night rather than partners, days when I know I'm not the easiest person to live with.

But what I've discovered in Andy—and what I didn't experience growing up—is someone who never dismisses my ideas, never calls my dreams unrealistic, and consistently shows up with unconditional love for our family. He's taught me what emotional presence looks like, what it means to prioritize relationships alongside work, and what it feels like to be truly supported. I know not everyone has this kind of partnership, and I don't take it for granted. I also know that having a supportive spouse doesn't erase the inner work I've had to do or make expansion automatic—it just means I'm not navigating that growth alone.

For years, I felt my childhood experiences were limitations holding me back—perhaps explaining why I constantly strive to achieve, constantly try to prove I'm enough. Through therapy, I've learned to confront these patterns and recognize they're simply part of my story. They don't make me good or bad—they're just threads in the tapestry of who I am.

For anyone reading this, I know you've experienced your battles, your wounds, your struggles. Whether you were raised in a broken household, witnessed a bitter divorce, had addiction affect your life, battled an eating disorder, felt unsupported in your dreams, or carried wounds that seem "smaller" than others—we all have our limitations. We all have moments that have made us feel constrained.

But these experiences, as painful as they may be, are also what shape us into the resilient, compassionate, and unique individuals we are today. They become part of our story, and when we learn to embrace and learn from them, they can be transformed from limitations into sources of strength and wisdom.

THE POWER OF OUR STORIES

Stories are 22 times more memorable and powerful than facts[1]. Your story matters. Your struggles matter. Just because your story may not seem as dramatic as someone else's doesn't mean it isn't valid, doesn't mean it hasn't shaped you, doesn't mean it isn't worthy of acknowledgement and healing.

Stop playing the comparison game with your pain. Stop minimizing your experiences because someone else "had it worse." Your story is yours to honor, to learn from, and to use as fuel for your expansion.

Here's something crucial I want you to understand about these stories: our limitations aren't really about the circumstances we face—they're about the stories we tell ourselves about those circumstances. The narrative we create becomes either the cage that constrains us or the foundation that propels us forward.

For years, I told myself a story about not being enough. Not thin enough, not accomplished enough, not worthy enough of my father's attention. These stories became the invisible boundaries of my life, the lines I was afraid to cross.

That's the insidious nature of inner limitations. Unlike external obstacles that we can see and strategize around, inner limitations operate below the surface. They're the silent saboteurs that whisper "you can't" when opportunity knocks, "you don't deserve this" when success appears, "this isn't meant for someone like you" when dreams beckon.

As Jamie Kern Lima teaches in her transformative book *WORTHY*, "You don't rise to what you believe is possible, you fall to what you believe you're worthy of."[2] Jamie Kern Lima's story is absolutely remarkable—she built IT Cosmetics from nothing and sold it to L'Oreal in a billion-dollar deal after facing rejection after rejection. She didn't give up when many others would have because she believed in herself.

We don't plateau at the edge of our capabilities—we plateau at the edge of what we believe we deserve. And that line? It's not drawn by our circumstances, our background, or our bank account. It's drawn by us, in our own minds, often in invisible ink we don't even realize we're using.

Worthiness isn't something you earn through achievement or validation from others. It's something you claim. It's a decision you make about yourself, *for* yourself. And the moment you make that decision—the moment you decide you're worthy of more—your life will change for the better.

There was a moment in therapy when my therapist asked me, "What would happen if you stopped trying to prove your worth?" The question struck me like lightning. What if I didn't need to achieve to be worthy? What if I was already enough? What if my value wasn't tied to my accomplishments, my appearance, or anyone else's validation?

That question began a journey of confronting my inner limitations—all those beliefs that had silently guided my choices for decades. It wasn't easy. It *isn't* easy. It's ongoing work. But with each layer I peel back, with each limiting belief I challenge, I find more freedom, more authenticity, more capacity to expand.

I'll never forget my first therapy session after my assault. I was scared to even talk. This therapist was supposed to be exceptional for trauma, but when I arrived, I didn't want to go in. Her office was in a basement, and I felt every emotion flood my body as I entered that back room with its old leather chair and more books than the New York Public Library.

During that session, she asked me to do an exercise. "Draw a house," she said. I thought she was crazy and almost walked out. But as I drew, I discovered more than I ever expected.

She asked me to describe the basement of my house. "Dark, dirty, messy," I said. As she unpacked this with me, she explained that this represented my repressed past—things I'd pushed into the basement, not wanting to talk about them, leaving them unresolved.

Although I only saw her for a few months, I'll never forget this exercise. She reminded me that we can't keep pushing the past away. When we talked about my attic—bright, open, and airy—she said that was where I was headed. But until I cleaned out the basement, I could never move completely forward.

So take a moment to consider: what does *your* basement look like?

Breaking out of these mental cages requires more than positive thinking or affirmations. It requires a systematic approach to identifying, challenging, and dismantling the beliefs that keep you small.

IDENTIFYING YOUR INVISIBLE CAGES

Most of our limiting beliefs sound so reasonable that we don't even recognize them as limitations. Research shows that many core beliefs about ourselves and the world form during early childhood, often before age 7, laying the foundation for how we interpret life.[3]

Some of these interpretations sound like common sense:

"I'm not good with numbers." (Really? Or did someone tell you that once and you believed them?)

"I'm not a people person." (Or did you just have some awkward social experiences and decide this was your identity?)

"I could never start my own business." (Says who? Based on what evidence?)

"I'm too old to change careers." (Compared to what standard?)

Most of us don't realize we're walking around with invisible cages, but here's how to spot them:

- **Listen to your language.** Pay attention to the phrases that follow "I am," "I can't," "I don't," or "I never." Those words often reveal the beliefs that keep you small.
- **Notice your automatic no's.** When opportunities arise, do you immediately think of reasons you *can't* do it? Those snap rejections are red flags for deeper limitations.
- **Examine your comfort zone.** What conversations, activities, or experiences do you consistently avoid? What story do you tell yourself about why they "aren't for you"?
- **Track your excuses.** Patterns in your excuses point to patterns in your thinking. Do you always cite the same reason—time, money, talent—for not moving forward?

Invisible cages are sneaky. You don't see them until you run into the bars. But once you know where they are, you have a choice: stay inside or start planning your escape.

A prison break takes courage, strategy, and relentless self-compassion. Here's how to begin:

- **Name the bars.** Limitations that stay unnamed keep their power. Journaling, therapy, or honest conversations help drag them into the light where they can't hide.
- **Challenge the story.** Ask yourself: *Is this actually true? Where did I learn it? Does it serve me now, or is it just an old script on repeat?*
- **Defy it with action.** Small, consistent steps create new evidence. If you "can't lead," start by leading one small project. If you "can't manage money," track your spending for a week. Action dismantles lies.
- **Upgrade your circle.** Research shows you become 15% more successful simply by being around people who raise your game. Proximity to ambition is contagious. Surround yourself with expanders, not limiters.
- **Practice self-compassion.** Remember—those cages were built as protection. They once kept you safe. Thank them for serving their purpose, and then outgrow them.

The work of confronting inner limitations isn't a one-time event. It's an ongoing practice of awareness, challenge, action, and compassion. Some days, you'll feel like you've broken through completely. Other days, those old limitations will resurface with surprising strength. That's normal. That's human.

What matters isn't that you overcome your limitations perfectly or permanently. What matters is that you keep showing up, keep questioning, keep expanding beyond what feels comfortable or safe.

Your limitations are not your destiny unless you decide they are.

I could have allowed my past experiences to limit my expectations for my own life. I could have accepted that certain types of relationships, certain levels of success, certain ways of being weren't available to me. I could have stayed within the comfortable confines of what felt safe and familiar.

But that would have meant sacrificing the expansive life that waited beyond those self-imposed boundaries. That would have meant continuing to live according to stories written by circumstance rather than authoring my own narrative.

So I made a choice—the same choice that's available to you right now. I chose to acknowledge my limitations but refuse to be defined by them. I chose to see them not as walls but as doorways—portals to greater understanding, compassion, and strength. I chose to believe that I was meant for more than the boundaries I had placed around my own life.

That choice doesn't erase the past. It doesn't eliminate the work of growth. But it opens up possibilities that simply don't exist when we allow our limitations to have the final word.

Your cages are not as strong as you think they are. And you are far more powerful than you've been led to believe.

AUDACITY IN ACTION CHALLENGE

This week, I challenge you to practice limitation disruption:

Identify: Choose one inner limitation that consistently holds you back from expansion. Be specific—not just "I'm afraid to take risks" but "I believe I'm not qualified enough to apply for leadership positions."

Design: Create a small, specific action that directly challenges this limitation. The action should be uncomfortable but not overwhelming—just enough to create a new experience that contradicts your limiting belief.

Practice: For one week, commit to taking this action daily (or as frequently as applicable). Document what happens, how you feel, and what you learn each time.

Reflect: At the end of the week, write about how this experience has impacted your relationship with this limitation. Has it weakened? Transformed? What new possibilities do you see?

SHARE YOUR JOURNEY

✹ "I'm confronting the inner limitations that have kept me playing small. This week I'm challenging my belief that [your limitation] by [your action]. What limitation are you ready to break through? #AudaciousExpansion"

Chapter 10:

UNFOLLOW TO FLY

*Life is what happens around you as you're busy
scrolling through your phone.*

Most mornings, we wake up and before meditation, before
the coffee, sometimes even before brushing our teeth, we
grab our phones and dive headfirst into everyone else's
highlight reel.

Within thirty seconds, we're comparing our bedhead to
someone's professional blowout. Our messy kitchen to their
staged breakfast spread. Our Monday morning dread to their
"living my best life" caption.

Without realizing it, we've already decided we're losing
at life—and we haven't even gotten out of bed yet.

We've become more connected than ever through
technology, yet somehow we're more disconnected from

reality than ever before. The average person checks their phone 96 times a day (that's once every ten minutes while awake—yikes!)[1], and the average young adult is on it more than seven hours per day.[2] That's nearly half their waking hours staring at a screen instead of living their actual life.

Do we actually know what these people are going through? Can we see the twenty takes it took to get that "perfect" photo? Are we watching their real life or their personal marketing campaign?

Get this: 60% of people say social media damages their self-esteem[3]. Sixty percent! That's not a *you* problem—that's a *we* problem. And I am guilty of it too. Believe me.

Social media is basically reality TV, except we're all the stars and the audience at the same time. We post the eighteenth photo with the perfect filter, not the outtakes where we look like we haven't slept in three days (because we haven't). We craft our online personas like Madison Avenue ad execs, showing only what sells the story we want people to believe.

FINDING YOUR LANE IN THE NOISE

Look, I'm not innocent here. But I try to share as openly as I can, especially in my stories, showing the realness and the rawness. Why? Because I truly believe you become the most audacious version of yourself when you're willing to share authentically.

I post about the rejections I face, the speaking gigs I don't land, the challenging days with my kids, and yes, even the challenges with marriage. I lean toward transparency rather than perfection because that's where real connection happens. But let's be honest—even my "real" moments are still curated to some degree. I'm choosing what to share and when.

So while I strive for authenticity, I'm still creating an incomplete picture of my life, just like everyone else. The difference? I'm trying to show the messy middle, not just the highlight reel. And when I do that, something magical happens—other people feel permission to be real too.

But here's the kicker: even with all my attempts at authenticity, I still fall into the comparison trap. I'll be scrolling, see another speaker with a bigger stage, and think, "What am I doing wrong?" Because that's what this stuff does to us—it makes us forget we're only seeing someone's greatest hits album, not their behind-the-scenes footage.

And let's be real—this goes way beyond Instagram. It's the colleague who seems to glide through promotions while you're grinding. It's the perfectly put-together mom at school pickup while you're running on fumes and dry shampoo. It's the couple at the restaurant who looks madly in love while you and your partner are discussing complicated life logistics.

Here's what I know for damn sure: there's only one person you can actually control in this whole mess, and that's you. I've spent way too much time looking at people "ahead" of me, but what does "ahead" even mean? Ahead according to whose timeline? Whose definition of success? Whose completely arbitrary measuring stick?

Let me remind you of a liberating truth: perfection doesn't exist, and you will always be enough, especially when you show up as your authentic self. When we awaken to our true nature and genuine sense of belonging, we naturally step away from the comparison game. We begin showing up as the best version of ourselves today—not as someone we saw online or sitting across from us at a meeting. That's when the magic truly unfolds.

Here's a perfect example of what I mean: This year, I participated in a parent act at our kids' school lip sync show. We went all out—dancing to 80s music, wearing ridiculous outfits, and showing up as the boldest, most unapologetic version of ourselves. Was it over the top? Absolutely. Did some other parents probably think we were crazy? Probably. Did we care? Not one bit.

What struck me most was how difficult it was to find other parents willing to participate. So many declined, worried about looking foolish or what people might think. But while they were sitting in the audience concerned about judgment, we were on stage having the time of our lives, creating memories our kids will never forget.

Most people are so trapped by the fear of comparison and judgment that they miss out on pure joy and authentic expression. They're so busy worrying about how they measure up that they forget to show up at all.

And here's the thing about "measuring up"—we're all measuring against different rulers, different timelines, different definitions of success. We've forgotten that there's no universal timeline for achievement, no standard schedule for when good things should happen in our lives.

Consider these powerful truths: Mark Zuckerberg became a billionaire in his twenties, while Vera Wang didn't design her first dress until she was forty. Morgan Freeman got his big acting break at fifty-two, while Zendaya became a household name as a teenager. Serena Williams won her first Grand Slam at seventeen and her most recent at thirty-five, proving success can span decades. Colonel Sanders started KFC at sixty-five, after a lifetime of setbacks. Obama retired from the presidency at fifty-five, while Trump began his at seventy. Some people celebrate twenty years of marriage, while others find their soulmate at fifty.

Life isn't a race; it's a journey where everyone operates in their own time zone. Some people may appear ahead of you—that's acceptable. Others might seem behind you—that's fine too. We're all swimming in our own races, in our own lanes, at our own pace. There's no need to envy or judge others; they're living according to their timeline, just as you're living according to yours.

Discovering your authentic path—your "swim lane"—isn't easy, but it's essential. One of the best ways to find it is to pay attention to joy. Spend the next month journaling each morning about what lights you up and makes you feel energized. What activities make you eager to start your day? Those are clues. Those are your swim lanes.

As Amberly Lago writes in her book *Joy Through the Journey: Shift Your Mindset, Embrace the Present Moment, and Cultivate Resilience Through Life's Ups and Downs*, joy isn't just a fleeting emotion—it's a compass. It points you back to creativity, resilience, and purpose.[1]

For me, joy was found in speaking and empowering women. Joy was showing up as my most audacious self, which felt intimidating after coming from the structured engineering world where I was expected to create precise calculations and follow established principles. This new direction felt different and edgy.

What I discovered, however, was that I didn't have to choose. I could be both a mother and a speaker. I could work as an engineer while appearing on stage in gold boots. I could wear a hard hat in the morning and podcast headphones in the afternoon. You can embrace these seemingly contradictory aspects of yourself too, but first you need to identify which lanes align with your core passions.

My advice is to select two to three things that genuinely excite you. You can always evolve and change direction later, but I've learned from experience that trying to occupy too many lanes simultaneously leads nowhere. A confused mind accomplishes nothing. We delay our progress when we spread ourselves too thin, attempting to be everywhere at once with limited resources.

You need to pick your lanes and stay in them. I'm talking about three areas, max (above and beyond being a parent, keeping up with the house, etc). Three areas that excite you. I truly believe that trying to juggle more than three swim lanes in your life is a recipe for mediocrity.

This year, I made a choice. My three audacious goals—above and beyond the non-negotiables like maintaining my core responsibilities—were the Audacious Summit, speaking, and writing this book. That's it. Everything else? It had to wait. Not forever. But not right now.

Was it hard to say no to other opportunities? Absolutely. But when you try to be everywhere, you end up being nowhere. Protect the time you dedicate to these priorities like your life depends on it. Find space each day to nurture these passions, even if it's just fifteen minutes.

I've never embraced standardized tests like the SATs that supposedly determine college destinies. These assessments, which you might take once, twice, or three times if particularly determined, significantly influence your life's trajectory but fail to measure your full potential.

Instead, I believe in establishing authentic benchmarks—personalized standards for measuring your wins and progress that align with your unique direction. We often adopt benchmarks created by others, but do these external standards actually motivate us? Do they inspire us to begin each day with enthusiasm and work diligently toward our goals?

The most effective benchmarks are those you create yourself—authentic milestones that challenge you appropriately, align with your values, and lead you toward meaningful success. When we place excessive pressure on ourselves through unrealistic standards, we risk burnout. I'm not suggesting you avoid hard work or committed effort, but your goals should be tangible and attainable while still stretching your capabilities.

We typically make one of two mistakes with goal-setting: either creating goals so ambitious that they paralyze us with their magnitude, or setting goals so modest that they fail to inspire meaningful growth. Your benchmarks should carefully balance challenge and achievability, pushing you forward without overwhelming you.

However, even when we set our own benchmarks, it can be difficult to avoid falling into the trap of comparison. But as we've discussed, comparison can be a dangerous game that undermines our sense of self-worth and progress.

So how do we actually accomplish this shift away from comparison? The reality is that comparison is deeply ingrained in human nature. While I haven't found a perfect solution, I've learned that comparison, when channeled differently, can actually elevate us. Instead of using comparison to measure our deficiencies, we can use it as a pathway to collaboration—learning how someone moved from point A to point B by listening to their podcast, reading their book, or understanding their journey through conversation.

Even as we work to reframe comparison in a more positive light, we may still find ourselves grappling with another common challenge: the fear of missing out, or FOMO.

In a world of constant connectivity and endless opportunities, it's easy to feel like we're always one decision away from a life-changing moment or experience.

I've experienced intense FOMO myself—worrying about missing events, games, networking opportunities, and potential connections. Though I've gradually learned to say no, I still feel that twinge of anxiety, that nagging worry that I might miss the perfect opportunity to secure a speaking engagement or make a valuable business contact.

Surprisingly, saying no has actually given me grace. I've discovered that the universe operates in mysterious ways, and declining one opportunity often creates space for something more aligned with my priorities.

Last year I faced this challenge with a wellness event in Arizona. I needed to be with my team there, but attending would have meant sacrificing important family time. I agonized over the decision, consumed by worry—though as I often remind myself, 90% of our worries never materialize.

What I realized after declining was that I didn't actually miss anything consequential. Instead, I gained precious time with my family and reinforced the priority of putting them before work, which I sometimes struggle with as a self-admitted workaholic.

This year, I attended that same wellness event but adjusted my schedule—flying out a day later so I could attend my daughter's lip-sync show first. I managed to fulfill both commitments by prioritizing what mattered most and finding creative solutions. Sometimes we don't need to completely decline opportunities but can instead find ways to adapt and accommodate our most important values.

This represents the shift from FOMO (Fear of Missing Out) to JOMO (Joy of Missing Out)—recognizing that declining constant comparison and external validation creates space for authentic presence in your own life. It means finding contentment in your choices rather than anxiety about what you might be missing.

JOMO isn't about withdrawal or isolation but intentional selection. It means being so present and engaged in your chosen activities that you feel no pull toward what you've declined. It's creating a life so aligned with your values that missing experiences that don't serve those values becomes a celebration of clarity rather than a source of regret.

Comparison can either be a thief or a teacher. Left unchecked, it steals our joy, drains our energy, and distorts our reality. But when we take back control, comparison can actually sharpen us, expand our vision, and fuel our growth.

Here are three powerful ways to reset your relationship with comparison:

1. Protect your inputs.

Set digital boundaries that give your mind room to breathe. Try a simple practice—like no social media for the first hour of your day, or a mini detox one day a week. I started by unplugging for the last 15 minutes of my power walks, and WOW—the difference was immediate. Just me, nature, and my mind allowed me to think and grow. And when you *do* engage online, curate intentionally. Follow people who inspire you, unfollow those who consistently trigger comparison or self-doubt.

2. Reframe your thoughts.

Comparison thrives in half-truths and highlight reels. The next time you feel that sting, pause and ask: *Am I seeing their whole reality—or just the shiny surface? Would I actually want their entire life, or am I romanticizing one piece of it?* And remember: we all move in different time zones. When you feel "behind," ask: *According to whose schedule? What am I learning here that will serve me later?*

3. Reconnect with what matters.

When comparison pulls you off course, anchor yourself back to your purpose. Ask: *Does this thought serve my mission? Am I being distracted from what really matters to me? What one action right now would pull me back into alignment?* And if someone triggers comparison, flip it into connection. Reach out. Ask about their journey. Turn envy into insight, and watch comparison transform into collaboration.

The goal isn't to erase comparison. It's to compare *wisely—* selectively, intentionally, and in ways that fuel expansion instead of contraction.

AUDACITY IN ACTION CHALLENGE

This week, pick *one* reset to practice:

- **Digital Detox:** Try a 24-hour social media fast. Notice what shifts—anxiety, relief, boredom, creativity—and journal your reflections.
- **Swim Lane Clarification:** Spend a little time each day writing down what brings you joy. By week's end, create a simple "This Is My Lane" list.
- **JOMO Experiment:** Say no to one thing you'd normally say yes to out of FOMO. Replace it with something that aligns with your true priorities.

Pick one. That's it. No extra credit for doing all three. The win here is not in proving, but in practicing. Practicing freedom. Practicing presence. Practicing joy in *your* lane.

SHARE YOUR JOURNEY

⚅ "I'm breaking free from the comparison trap by staying in my lane and defining my own success metrics. What's your unique swim lane? #AudaciousExpansion"

Part 3:

EXPANDING INTO ACTION

Don't forget to download your free journal before continuing.

Chapter 11:

BE BOLD. STAY BOLDER.

Belief is not about feeling ready; it's about taking action despite your doubts.

Now it's time for the fun part, where the rubber hits the road...

Throughout this book, we've explored various aspects of living in audacious expansion. Now it's time to bring it all together into a practical framework I call the BOLD Method.

This isn't some fluffy motivational poster hanging in your cubicle. This is a battle-tested strategy. This is your tactical manual for transformation. Think of me as your drill sergeant for audacity—I'm going to give you the tools, the training, and the tough love to make this stick.

Just like we're audacious, sometimes we have to be bold, sometimes we have to be brave, and most days, that's how we need to operate to navigate life's trials and tribulations.

But being bold isn't always easy. Showing up authentically isn't always the simplest recipe, which is where the BOLD method comes into play.

B STANDS FOR BELIEVE IN YOURSELF (EVEN WHEN NO ONE ELSE DOES!)

Mission: Build unshakeable self-belief through evidence and action.

Because that's where it starts—with you. If we don't have a mechanism to believe in ourselves when everything else seems to be crumbling around us, when self-doubt kicks in, when those little voices whisper, "Who do you think you are trying to accomplish this goal or dream"—how will you champion yourself?

Belief is not a feeling you wait for; it's a decision you make. Every damn day. And like any muscle, it gets stronger with use.

O REPRESENTS OWN YOUR PROCESS (CONSISTENCY IS YOUR SUPERPOWER!)

Mission: Create non-negotiable systems that work with your authentic self, not against it.

I truly believe that consistency is the number one recipe for success—but it has to be *your* version of consistency.

Showing up every day in ways that honor your natural rhythms while still being strategic about your actions despite the excuses, the mistakes, the days when you quite frankly, "just don't want to do it." When I say consistency, it has to be the right actions for *you*—actions that push you toward your goals in ways that feel sustainable and authentic.

Owning the process means you control what you can control and let go of what you can't, but you do it in a way that aligns with who you actually are. You can't control if the client says yes, but you can control making the call in your own authentic style. You can't control if you get the promotion, but you can control showing up prepared every day in ways that leverage your unique strengths.

L STANDS FOR LEAN ON OTHERS (YOUR CIRCLE IS YOUR STRENGTH!)

Mission: Build a strategic support network that accelerates your growth.

Jim Rohn famously said you're the average of the five people you spend the most time with. But I believe it goes deeper: your resilience is shaped by the strength of your circle.

Contrary to networking events and collecting business cards, this step is about strategically building your personal board of directors—people who have different strengths, perspectives, and expertise that complement your journey.

D REPRESENTS DEVELOP OTHERS (MULTIPLY YOUR IMPACT!)

Mission: Create a legacy by lifting others as you climb.

The final component of BOLD might seem counterintuitive. When we're focused on our own growth and expansion, why think about developing others? Because this is where the magic happens. When you develop others, your own learning deepens, your purpose expands, your impact multiplies, your resilience strengthens, and your legacy builds.

How am I investing in someone else? Who am I surrounding myself with? Who am I lifting up? Because I truly believe that when we operate in gratitude and show others what's possible, remarkable things start to happen.

THE POWER OF INTEGRATION

The real power of BOLD emerges when all four elements work together: Belief fuels your commitment to the process. Owning the process builds evidence for belief. Leaning on others strengthens your resolve. Developing others deepens your own growth.

Before we dive into this more, let me share how I've seen this play out in my own life. After my assault, belief was my biggest challenge. The trauma had shaken my foundation, leaving me questioning everything I thought I knew about myself and the world. I had to deliberately rebuild my belief muscle through daily affirmations, evidence-gathering, and surrounding myself with people who believed in me when I couldn't believe in myself.

As *belief* began to strengthen, I could focus more on the ongoing process—creating new routines that reinforced my security and agency and developing *consistent habits* that helped me reclaim my power day by day. I leaned heavily on my *support system* during this time, allowing myself to be vulnerable about my struggles instead of trying to handle everything alone.

Perhaps most healing of all was when I began to *develop others*—sharing my story with women who had experienced similar traumas, offering the understanding that only comes from walking a similar path. Each time I helped someone else take a step forward in their healing journey, my own resilience deepened.

That's the transformative power of BOLD. It's a framework for becoming the person who can withstand life's greatest challenges and still move forward with purpose and strength.

I want to remind you that being bold and using this method doesn't mean every single day you have to show up with your Superman or Superwoman cape on. It means being willing to return to a method when you feel off track, when things aren't aligned, or when things aren't going your way.

In the coming chapters, we'll dive deeper into each element, giving you specific tools and strategies to build unshakeable belief, create sustainable systems, build your support network, and multiply your impact through developing others.

But transformation starts with a single step. Which element of BOLD calls to you first?

AUDACITY IN ACTION CHALLENGE

This week, choose one element of BOLD to focus on:

- **Believe:** Write down three pieces of evidence that you're capable of achieving a goal that currently feels impossible
- **Own:** Identify one daily action you could take consistently toward your biggest aspiration
- **Lean:** Reach out to one person who could offer guidance or support in an area where you're growing
- **Develop:** Share something you've learned with someone who could benefit from your experience

Start with whichever element feels most needed in your life right now. Notice how focusing on just one component begins to strengthen the others.

SHARE YOUR JOURNEY

✸ "Taking my first BOLD step this week by [specific action]. I'm ready to turn expansion into lasting change. #AudaciousExpansion"

Chapter 12:

BET WILDLY ON YOU

*Belief doesn't require feeling ready — it requires
only the courage to begin.*

It was June 2010. The summer heat index was breaking records, and there I was, trying to shave eighty seconds off my mile time for the upcoming marathon. Every morning, I'd watch three men at the gym—racing, sprinting, working with an intensity that made my efforts feel amateur in comparison. They moved with such grace, such effortless power. Meanwhile, there I was: beat red, gasping for air, more of a fast power walker with ambition than a real runner.

Every day, the same thought would cross my mind: "Do you think they'd let me join them?"

And every day, I'd quickly dismiss it. They were too fast, too focused, too professional. They were in a different league entirely. Until one day, something shifted. Maybe it was exhaustion from fighting my own self-doubt. Maybe it was audacity finally winning over fear. Whatever it was, I found myself walking up to them after their workout.

"Hi, do you think... could I run with you?"

After a moment of eye contact exchanges among them and a few chuckles, they said, "Sure. Be here tomorrow at 5 AM. We're doing fifteen miles."

Did I feel ready? No. Did I feel worthy? No. Did I feel terrified? Absolutely. But belief is not about feeling ready; it's about taking action despite your doubts.

For the next eight weeks, I showed up at 4:45 AM on weekdays with a headlamp. I showed up on long Saturdays for grueling fifteen, eighteen, twenty-one-mile runs. I showed up through pouring rain and sweltering heat. And often I felt like a lost puppy chasing the pack.

Every single day, the voices in my head would say: "What are you doing?" "You don't belong here!" "You're slowing them down!" "You're making a fool of yourself!"

But every single day, I made a choice to believe in the possibility of more than what those voices were telling me.

When marathon day arrived, I wasn't just physically transformed—I was mentally transformed. I crossed the finish line with my best time yet, shaving almost a minute and a half off my mile. But the real victory wasn't in the time improvement. It was in what I learned about belief.

I learned something that every athlete knows but most people forget: the starting line is where champions are made, not the finish line.

BUILDING YOUR BELIEF BANK ACCOUNT

See, those runners didn't become fast because they felt confident. They became confident because they kept showing up to the starting line, day after day, regardless of how they felt. Every morning at 5 AM was another starting line. Every tough workout was another starting line. Every race was another starting line.

That's what I call the Starting Line Mindset—the understanding that confidence isn't something you wait around for before you begin; it's something you build by beginning.

We all have that inner critic. It tells you you're not ready, not good enough, that everyone's watching you fail. Those voices are like that person at the gym who dishes out unsolicited advice—loud, persistent, and utterly convinced they know better than you.

But you don't quiet the critic by debating with it. You quiet it by moving anyway.

When my alarm went off at 4 AM, the voice was always there, reminding me of all the reasons I didn't belong. So I didn't argue. I laced up my shoes. Step by step, action by action, the voice faded—not because I convinced it, but because I proved to myself what was possible.

That's the gift of the starting line. It doesn't care if you feel ready. It simply asks: Will you show up?

Because the heaviest barriers aren't out in the world—they're in our minds. And they love to masquerade as "reasonable." They sound like: I'm not experienced enough. I don't have the right background. I'm too old/young/busy/broke.

The truth is, those aren't facts. They're fears. Fear disguised as pragmatism. The most dangerous limits are the ones we've absorbed so deeply we mistake them for reality. When that happens, we stop expanding. We shrink. We overwork, we exhaust ourselves, and still the opportunities slip through our fingers like sand.

Think of belief as a muscle that requires regular training. Just like you can't expect to run a marathon without consistent training, you can't expect to believe in your expansion without consistent practice. Belief isn't just a feeling—it's a discipline. It's a choice we make daily that transforms how we show up in the world.

Belief doesn't require feeling ready—it requires only the courage to begin. When I approached those runners, I wasn't ready. I was terrified. But I asked anyway. Belief grows through action—not through thinking, planning, or waiting. Every morning I showed up to run, even when I felt like the slowest person there, I was building belief through action. Belief strengthens through consistency—showing up when the novelty wears off. Week three of those brutal morning runs? That's when belief really started to build, when it stopped being exciting and started being a commitment.

Belief expands through challenge—becoming unshakeable in the face of obstacles. The harder those runs got, the stronger my belief in my own capacity became. And belief multiplies through community—finding others who see your potential when you can't.

Think of belief as a bank account that requires regular deposits. Just like you can't withdraw money you haven't deposited, you can't withdraw confidence during challenging times if you haven't made consistent deposits during easier ones. Daily deposits might include acknowledging effort rather than just outcomes, celebrating small wins along the way, recognizing growth even when it's messy, choosing courage over comfort in small moments, and surrounding yourself with people who believe in your expansion.

Let's be real: belief isn't constant. There will be days when you wake up questioning everything. Days when others seem to surpass you effortlessly. Days when the path forward feels unclear and the voices of doubt are deafening. Those are precisely the moments when belief matters most.

I had one of those moments of doubt recently. I was scrolling through social media and saw post after post of women my age who seemed to have it all figured out. Bigger audiences, fancier stages, more impressive accomplishments. I spiraled into that familiar place of "I'm not enough."

Then I remembered something: my belief in myself must be stronger than my circumstances. It must be so deeply rooted that it doesn't waver when I'm faced with comparison or challenge. So I closed my phone, opened my Audacious

Badass List, and reminded myself of my own journey. Not to compare, but to reconnect with my own evidence of expansion and growth.

Believing in yourself is not selfish—it's one of the most generous gifts you can give to the world. When you truly believe in your capacity to expand, you naturally take actions aligned with that belief. You see opportunities others miss. You persevere when others quit. You recover more quickly from setbacks. You give others permission to believe in their own expansion.

Your audacious belief becomes a beacon for others still trapped in their limiting beliefs. By fully believing in yourself, you create a ripple effect that expands far beyond your individual journey. I think about those runners who let me join them. They didn't just change my marathon time— they changed my understanding of what was possible. They believed I could keep up before I believed it myself. And now, every time I encourage someone else to take a leap they're not sure they're ready for, I'm paying that forward.

Belief is about action in the presence of doubt. It's about showing up when the voices say "stay home." It's about trying when logic says "play safe." It's about asking the question even when you're terrified of the answer.

Those runners didn't make me faster. They simply provided the space for me to discover my own strength. Your belief is waiting for you to do the same. Expansion is never a straight line. It's messy, chaotic, and sometimes feels impossible. There will be days when you question everything. But those are precisely the moments when belief matters most.

Let me be clear that believing in your expansion isn't about denying reality or convincing yourself of falsehoods. It's about recognizing that the boundaries of what's possible for you are far more expansive than your mind would have you believe. Your belief creates your reality. Choose wisely.

What will you choose to believe in today?

AUDACITY IN ACTION CHALLENGE

This week, find your version of approaching the runners. Find something that scares you just enough to make you grow, and take one concrete step toward it. Identify one area where you've been playing small because of self-doubt.

Using your Audacious Badass List as fuel, take one concrete action step beyond your comfort zone. Document what happens—not just the outcome, but how you felt before, during, and after.

SHARE YOUR JOURNEY

✺ "Today I chose belief over doubt. What scary step are you ready to take? #AudaciousExpansion"

Chapter 13:

OWN YOUR OWN FLAVOR OF CRAZY

The very experiences that once felt like setbacks often become the foundation for your greatest contributions.

Sometimes, taking that first step toward a goal isn't about doing something big and flashy out in the world—it's about turning inward. We expand when we stop downplaying our brilliance and learn to fully claim what makes us unique.

My son Drew started playing baseball later than most kids on his team. When he made it to the travel team, he quickly realized he wasn't the strongest player—not because he lacked athletic ability, but simply because he hadn't put in the same number of reps as the other kids.

He was particularly frustrated with his batting. Despite his strength and agility, he couldn't connect with the ball the way he wanted. My husband and I decided to hire a hitting coach.

I'll never forget the day that Nick, Drew's coach, said to him: "Listen, I'm gonna start recording you. We're gonna watch your swings. But guess what, Drew? You probably think I'm gonna tell you to focus on the things you're not doing right. But that's far from the truth. We're actually gonna focus on all the things you *are* doing right and perfect those."

That moment was an epiphany for me. How often do we obsess over fixing our weaknesses instead of amplifying our strengths? We pour energy into things that will never come naturally, when we could be expanding what we're already good at.

What if we focused on the swings that went right instead of the ones that didn't?

Your confidence to "do the thing" isn't going to magically appear like some fairy godmother situation. It grows through action, through doing the thing scared, through proving to yourself one small step at a time that you're capable of more than you imagined.

I think about my own journey. Two and a half years ago, I stepped on my first paid stage. Less than a year ago, I started writing this book. Word by word, page by page, voice note by voice note. And I recognize that none of this happened overnight. No one is an overnight success. We think in the world we're living in—this rat race—that everything happened yesterday, but we need to remind ourselves that it takes consistency. It takes the day in and day out action.

Especially the days when no one's watching us, especially the days when there's no applause, especially the days when we want to throw in the towel (and believe me, I have had *plenty*).

It takes owning who we are.

Let me tell you about the time I accidentally won a karaoke contest on a cruise ship. (Yes, you read that right, and no, I'm not making this up to sound cooler than I am.)

I'm on vacation, feeling relaxed and maybe a little too confident. I see the karaoke sign-up sheet and think, "What the heck, I'll throw my name in there. There's no way they'll pick me, and even if they do, how bad could it be?"

Friends, I am to singing what pineapple is to pizza— divisive at best, offensive at worst. I have the vocal range of a dying walrus with a head cold. This is not false modesty; this is a documented fact.

But guess what? They called my name. And in that moment, I had a choice: slink away in embarrassment or embrace my terrible singing with the enthusiasm of a Broadway star who forgot she can't actually sing.

I got up there and absolutely *owned* my awfulness. I sang off-key with so much confidence that the audience couldn't help but love it. I danced like nobody was watching (even though everyone definitely was). I turned my complete lack of talent into entertainment gold.

And I won. *I actually won.*

Not because I was the best singer—let's be clear, I was objectively the worst. But because I embraced my unique flavor of crazy with such authentic joy that it became contagious.

Here's why I'm telling you this ridiculous story: That karaoke moment taught me something important about showing up. For years, I thought "showing up" meant being the best, the fastest, the most prepared. I thought it meant earning applause through perfection.

But sometimes showing up means being willing to look foolish. Sometimes it means doing the thing badly but with your whole heart. Sometimes it means turning your weakness into your superpower simply by refusing to apologize for who you are. Sometimes it means showing my kids through a simple way that you are always enough and life is too short to be worried about what everyone else thinks of you.

That's what owning your process really looks like. It's not about being perfect or having all the skills. It's about showing up fully as yourself, embracing your quirks, and turning your perceived weaknesses into your secret weapons—consistently, whether anyone's watching or not.

We've talked a lot about the importance of consistency, but consistency without authenticity is just going through the motions. And authenticity without consistency is just a nice idea. Real expansion happens when you commit to showing up as your true self, day after day, with strategic intention.

So how do you actually define what your unique process looks like? How do you figure out what makes you different and turn that into your competitive advantage?

I like to compare this to how I've evolved my approach to fitness as I've gotten older. I used to think there was only one way to be "productive"—run hard, pound the pavement, push to exhaustion. If I wasn't sweating buckets, I didn't consider it worthwhile. I was trying to fit into someone else's definition of what fitness should look like.

The older I get, the more I realize that my best results come from honoring my natural rhythms. Some days I need to sprint, some days I need to walk, some days I need to rest. The key isn't following someone else's training plan—it's designing one that works with my body, my schedule, my energy patterns.

Your expansion process works the same way. Instead of copying what works for others, you need to identify what works uniquely for you.

Start with your natural patterns. Are you a morning person who thinks clearest at dawn, or a night owl who gets energized after dark? Do you work better in short bursts or long stretches? Do you process information by talking it through or by thinking quietly? Stop fighting your natural wiring and start designing around it.

Identify your unique strengths. What do people consistently come to you for? What feels effortless to you but challenging to others? What problems do you see solutions for that others miss? These are clues to your distinctive value.

Embrace your productive quirks. Maybe you think better while walking. Maybe you need music to focus. Maybe you work best with tight deadlines or maybe you need lots of buffer time. These are features to leverage.

Define your non-negotiables. What conditions do you absolutely need to do your best work? What drains your energy versus what fuels it? What boundaries do you need to maintain to stay in your zone of genius?

In the engineering world, we talk about the "Happy Path"—the ideal scenario where everything goes according to plan. But any seasoned professional knows this path rarely exists outside of textbooks. Your personal process isn't about finding the happy path—it's about building a system that works even when things go sideways.

When setbacks happen—and they will—having a process built around your authentic self means you can adapt without losing your core identity. You're not trying to be someone else; you're being the best version of yourself under changing circumstances.

The question I want you to consider is, do you have a process authentic enough to sustain you through obstacles? This is where is where owning your unique expansion process becomes your secret weapon.

One of my favorite ways to own your expansion process is what I call the **3-3-30 method**. This simple framework creates a foundation for consistent growth without requiring hours of your day. What makes this approach so powerful is that it works with your natural rhythms rather than against them, building sustainable momentum toward your most audacious goals.

Three minutes: Spend at least the first three minutes of your day investing in yourself—before emails, social media, or even that first cup of coffee (even longer than three minutes is even better!). This might be prayer or meditation to center yourself before the world starts making demands. Perhaps journaling to capture your thoughts before they're influenced by outside voices. Maybe reading to feed your mind with wisdom that elevates your thinking. Or intention setting to declare what you want from this day, not what it wants from you. Sometimes it's simply quiet reflection—being still and listening to your inner voice.

This is about presence. The first three minutes (or 0.2%) of your day are sacred ground where you establish how you'll show up for the next seven or eight hours. I've found that these initial moments create a ripple effect that influences every interaction, decision, and response throughout my day.

Three gratitudes: Write down three specific things you're grateful for—precise moments that anchor you in abundance. Not just "my family" but "the way my daughter squealed with laughter when I chased her around the kitchen island last night." Not just "my job" but "the colleague who sent me that encouraging message after yesterday's challenging meeting." Not just "my health" but "the strength in my legs that carried me through that difficult run when my mind wanted to quit."

This practice rewires your brain to scan for opportunities rather than obstacles. What's fascinating is how this simple habit shifts your perception throughout the day—suddenly you're noticing small victories and meaningful connections that would have otherwise passed by unnoticed.

Thirty minutes: Dedicate thirty minutes to your stretch goals—those audacious dreams that require consistent attention to become reality. This might be writing your book, where one page today means 365 pages by year's end. Perhaps building your business through small strategic actions that compound over time. Maybe learning new skills, where consistent practice beats sporadic cramming. Or developing relationships, since meaningful connections require regular investment. Whatever it is, your dreams won't build themselves without consistent effort.

Thirty minutes of focused attention moves you further than hours of distracted effort. The thirty minute component is so powerful because it's substantial enough to make meaningful progress but short enough to fit into even your busiest days. If needed, you can break this up into two fifteen-minute periods—as long as you make time for both! When you honor your commitment to yourself day after day, you're building belief in your capacity to achieve your goals.

The 3-3-30 method is thirty-six minutes—just 2% of your entire day—invested in owning your process. The beauty of this method is that it doesn't require a complete life overhaul or hours of additional work. It simply asks you to be intentional with a small fraction of your time. Don't tell me you can't find the time to do this but you can binge that Netflix series you're addicted to.

At the end of the day, it's your choice.

It's your choice to lace up the sneakers.

It's your choice to write the first word.

It's your choice to get on the first stage.

It's all up to you.

So my question to you: How are you going to make your big, audacious goals happen?

As James Clear illustrates in *Atomic Habits*, the compound effect of small improvements is powerful—mathematically, getting just 1% better each day would make you 37 times better over a year.[1] This is the compound effect of owning the process. What does 2% look like? One more page written. One more call made. One more minute of exercise. One more act of kindness. One more hour of sleep (yes, I said it). One more step toward your goal.

These small actions, when taken consistently and aligned with your authentic self, create the foundation for your audacious expansion. They won't always feel significant in the moment—rarely does transformation happen in dramatic, movie-worthy moments. Instead, it's built in the quiet discipline of showing up day after day as yourself, gradually expanding your capacity for growth, service, and impact.

Remember that expansion isn't about achievement, rather the focus is on alignment. When your actions, values, and authentic self-work in harmony, you create a resonance that amplifies your impact far beyond what you could accomplish through effort alone. This is sustainable expansion—the kind that doesn't lead to burnout or emptiness, but to deeper fulfillment and greater possibility.

Your 2% matters. Your unique approach matters. Your authentic self matters.

So let's get after it.

AUDACITY IN ACTION CHALLENGE

This week, design your unique expansion process:

Map Your Natural Patterns: For three days, track when you have the most energy, when you think most clearly, and when you feel most creative. Use this data to design your ideal daily rhythm instead of fighting against your natural flow.

Identify Your Distinctive Value: Write down three things people consistently come to you for advice about, three problems you see solutions for that others miss, and three ways you approach challenges differently than most people. These patterns reveal your unique strengths.

Design Your 3-3-30 Framework: Map out exactly what you'll do with your three minutes each morning (a specific meditation, affirmation, or journaling prompt), identify your three daily gratitudes format, and block thirty minutes in your calendar for focused work on your biggest expansion goal.

SHARE YOUR JOURNEY

⊛ "I'm designing my unique expansion process by honoring what makes me different instead of trying to fit someone else's mold. What's one way you work differently that might actually be your secret weapon? #AudaciousExpansion"

Chapter 14

CIRCLE UP, LEVEL UP

Your life is the most important enterprise you'll ever lead. It deserves strategic guidance.

I'll never forget the moment I realized the true power of connection. It wasn't at a high-powered networking event or a professional conference—it was on a rainy afternoon just before my sister's wedding.

My younger sister Kim and her "perfect match" Ryan had dreamed of a perfect Cape Cod beach wedding, with guests' toes in the sand and a breathtaking sunset over the water. Instead, on her wedding day, the skies opened up with a torrential downpour an hour before the ceremony. As she sat in the doorway in her wedding dress, visibly devastated, my newly three-year-old son Drew toddled over in his tiny blue seersucker suit. Without a word, he sat beside her, offering silent comfort. Then, to everyone's surprise, he ran outside and began splashing joyfully in the puddles, his formal clothes quickly soaked through.

In that simple act, this child taught us all something we needed to remember about life: storms will come, but it's how we choose to weather them that matters. And more importantly, it's who we weather them with that makes all the difference.

Over ten years later, this remains one of my most vivid memories of that day—not the fancy reception or even the ceremony itself, but this small moment of connection that showed us all how to expand rather than contract in the face of disappointment.

This is the essence of what I call "leaning into support systems." Our capacity to weather life's storms, celebrate its joys, and navigate its complexities is directly tied to the strength of the connections we cultivate.

BUILDING YOUR BOARD OF DIRECTORS

Jim Rohn famously said, "You're the average of the five people you spend the most time with." But I believe we need more than just a circle of influence—we need what I call a "Board of Directors" for life.

In the construction world, I've never seen a single person successfully manage a complex project alone. The most impressive builds require structural engineers, architects, project managers, specialists, and skilled tradespeople working in concert. Yet somehow, we approach the infinitely more complex project of building our lives as if we should handle every aspect independently.

Your life is the most important enterprise you'll ever lead. It deserves strategic guidance, diverse expertise, and unwavering support—just like any thriving organization.

Think about it: Every successful company has a board of directors—people with different expertise, perspectives, and experiences who help guide the organization's direction. Why should your life be any different?

A company would never stack its board with identical perspectives or redundant skill sets. Similarly, your personal board shouldn't just be filled with people who think exactly like you or only tell you what you want to hear. Diversity of thought, experience, and perspective is what makes a board truly valuable.

Your personal board should include people who can help you navigate different aspects of life: Who do you turn to for relationship advice? Who helps you make career decisions? Who challenges your thinking? Who holds you accountable? Who tells you the hard truths? Who celebrates your wins? Who picks you up after failures?

The key distinction between a social circle and a true board of directors lies in intentionality. These aren't just people you enjoy spending time with—though that matters too. These are people you *deliberately invite* into specific areas of your life because of what they bring to the table.

Your board should include people who provide different types of essential support:

Emotional supporters are the listeners and encouragers. These are the people who create safe spaces for vulnerability. They listen without rushing to solve, offer comfort without judgment, and validate your feelings without minimizing them. They're the ones you call on your worst days and your best days because they genuinely sit with you through your sorrows and celebrate your joys. Everyone needs at least one person who sees them completely and loves them anyway.

Strategic supporters serve as your mentors and advisors. These board members have walked paths similar to yours and can help you navigate the terrain ahead. They've made mistakes you haven't made yet and achieved successes you're still working toward. They offer practical wisdom, share relevant experiences, and help you see around corners you didn't know existed. Unlike emotional supporters, they're not afraid to push you beyond comfortable thinking.

Accountability supporters are your challengers and truth-tellers. Perhaps the most valuable and rarest members of your board, these are the people who love you enough to tell you what you need to hear, not just what you want to hear. They hold up mirrors when you're avoiding reflection. They question your excuses when you're justifying inaction. These relationships require profound trust and mutual respect—they can't function without both.

Growth supporters are your visionaries and connectors. These board members expand your sense of possibility. They see potential in you that you may not see in yourself. They connect you with opportunities, people, and resources that accelerate your growth. They're often the ones who say, "Have you ever considered..." or "I think you'd be perfect for..." These relationships energize and inspire you toward audacious goals you might otherwise dismiss as unrealistic.

The importance of having such a diverse board of directors was a lesson I learned the hard way during my first major project management role. I surrounded myself exclusively with people who validated my decisions and never questioned my approach—which was a terrible idea. When the project hit inevitable hurdles, I had no one in my circle who could offer alternative perspectives or specialized expertise. The project eventually succeeded, but at tremendous personal cost—stress, self-doubt, and burnout that could have been avoided with the right guidance.

But that wasn't my only mistake. I also made the error of keeping energy vampires in my circle far too long—people who constantly complained and never celebrated my wins. I told myself I was being loyal, but really I was just afraid of confrontation. The truth is, these relationships were slowly draining my confidence and limiting my growth. (I guess I should have read *LET THEM* a lot earlier in life.)

When examining your support system, consider the energy exchange: Who fills your cup? Who drains your energy? Who celebrates your wins? Who seems threatened by your success? Remember: if you look around and don't feel inspired by those in your circle, then it's not a circle—it's a cage.

This is why it's so important to be intentional about who gets access to your energy. If you have people in your life who consistently take more energy than they give, who don't support your dreams, or who make you feel smaller rather than bigger—it's time to create some distance. You don't owe anyone unlimited access to your energy, especially if they're not investing in your growth.

THE POWER OF QUALITY CONNECTIONS

Building genuine connections requires more than just collecting contacts. I used to approach networking events with a singular goal: collect as many business cards as possible. Success was measured by the number of hands shaken and contacts made. Now, I realize how misguided that approach was. True connection isn't about quantity—it's about quality. I'd rather make two or three meaningful connections than twenty shallow ones.

Instead of asking the standard questions about weather or work, I try to ask questions that light people up—questions about their future, their passion projects, what excites them. Research shows that when people talk about their passions, their brains release dopamine—the same chemical that makes us feel happy and motivated. So when you get someone talking about what truly matters to them, you're literally giving them a neurochemical reward while building a foundation for genuine connection.

I noticed the power of this attentive listening early in my relationship with my now-husband. During one of our first dates, he mentioned his love for different mustards, particularly wasabi mustard. For his birthday a few weeks later, I presented him with three different mustards, including a special-ordered wasabi variety.

It was a simple gift—probably seemed strange to the restaurant waitstaff—but thirteen years later, he still mentions it as one of his favorite presents ever. Not because of the mustard itself, but because I had truly listened and remembered something that mattered to him. This kind of attentiveness is the foundation of meaningful connection. It shows people that you see them—really see them—in a world where most of us feel invisible.

Another powerful form of connection is the kind that stands the test of time. I think of my oldest friend, Amy—not in age, but in duration. We've known each other since I attended her third birthday party. She lived next door, and though life took us in different directions—she stayed in our hometown while I moved away—our connection remains unbreakable and to this day, we still talk frequently.

What I treasure most about this friendship is that no matter how much time passes between conversations, we can always pick up right where we left off. There's no awkwardness, no formality—just the comfortable rhythm of a connection that's weathered decades.

Growing up, I experienced the beauty of homes where you could walk in without knocking, borrow an egg when you ran out mid-recipe, or perform backyard dance routines with neighbors who remain close friends decades later. This continued with what we later called the "Bungalow Village Gang"—several families who gathered annually at rustic cottages on Newfound Lake in New Hampshire.

The magic was in the community we formed. We even held "unbirthday" parties for all the children, singing "A very happy unbirthday to you" and lining up by age for a photo that became an annual tradition. Now, as adults with our own families, we still attend each other's weddings and recreate that lineup, carrying on a tradition that spans generations.

These early experiences taught me that community isn't something that happens accidentally—it's cultivated intentionally. The "Bungalow Moms" became second mothers to me, present for milestones from graduations to weddings to the birth of my children. These communities keep us grounded, supported, and connected to something larger than ourselves.

Leaning on others can be challenging because it requires vulnerability. You have to admit you don't have all the answers, risk rejection, show imperfection, ask for help, and be honest about struggles. But vulnerability isn't weakness—it's the ultimate form of strength. It's saying, "I value my growth more than my ego."

Ironically, the more successful people become, often the harder it is for them to lean on others. They're used to being the strong one, the one others come to for help. They feel pressure to have it all together, fear showing weakness, or have simply forgotten how to receive. Yet this is precisely when they need support the most.

Creating an effective support system isn't about collecting people—it's about cultivating relationships that enhance your expansion journey. This strategic approach requires honest assessment, clear intention, and consistent action.

Start by taking inventory of who's already influencing your life. Map your inner circle by writing down the names of the seven to ten people you interact with most frequently. For each person, identify their impact—do they primarily energize or drain you, challenge or comfort you, expand or limit your thinking? Assess coverage by determining which areas of your life receive adequate support and where the gaps exist.

After understanding your current support landscape, define your needs by identifying specific roles. Do you need a financial mentor? A wellness accountability partner? A creative collaborator? Clarify what's missing—perhaps you have plenty of encouragers but lack truth-tellers, or vice versa.

Once you've identified gaps, look beyond convenience—the right board members rarely enter your life by accident. You must intentionally seek them. Pursue meaningful connections by joining communities, organizations, or groups aligned with your values and aspirations. Create value first by approaching potential mentors with something valuable rather than immediately asking for help. Be specific with requests—when seeking advice or support, clearly articulate what you're looking for rather than making vague asks.

Building your board is just the beginning. Regular check-ins require scheduling intentional time with your key supporters—don't leave these vital relationships to chance. Express gratitude by acknowledging the specific ways board members impact your life. Reciprocate value, as support flows both ways—look for opportunities to contribute to your board members' growth.

The long-running Harvard Study of Adult Development reveals that the quality of our relationships—not fame, wealth, or career success—is the strongest predictor of both happiness and longevity.[1] Strong relationships also protect our mental health, lowering anxiety and depression while boosting self-esteem and empathy.[2] And the benefits aren't just emotional—our bodies respond physiologically to connection, releasing oxytocin, lowering stress hormones, and even strengthening immune function.

This is the beautiful paradox of support systems: the more you lean in, the stronger you become. And the stronger you become, the more you can support others in their expansion.

No one achieves greatness alone. Behind every successful person is a carefully cultivated network of support. The question isn't whether you need others—it's whether you're brave enough to let them in and wise enough to keep the energy vampires out.

AUDACITY IN ACTION CHALLENGE

This week, take these four steps to lean into your support systems:

1. **Reach Out:** Contact someone from your past with whom you've lost touch but who once provided valuable support. Simply say, "I was thinking about you today."
2. **Be Vulnerable:** Share a current struggle with someone you trust. Don't ask for solutions—just allow yourself to be seen in your imperfection.
3. **Notice Needs:** Pay attention to what makes the people in your life light up. Make notes in your phone about their preferences, dreams, and passions.

4. **Evaluate Energy:** Take an honest look at your relationships and identify any energy vampires. Consider what boundaries you might need to set or what distance you might need to create.

SHARE YOUR JOURNEY

✪ "Building my board of directors one relationship at a time. Who's on yours? #AudaciousExpansion"

Chapter 15:

LIGHT 'EM UP

*We weren't put here to play small. We were put
here to leave a legacy.*

Development—the "D" in our BOLD framework—is where
your personal expansion stops being just about you and
starts becoming rocket fuel for everyone around you.
When you develop others, you're not just growing yourself.
You're creating seismic ripple effects that can literally span
generations.

My biggest teacher in this comes from my daughter
Adelyn. One day when it was 87 degrees outside, she came
downstairs for her brother's football practice wearing her
Ms. Claus Christmas dress. Not because she was confused
about the season (though I briefly wondered), but because
that's what felt right to her that day. And you know what? She

wore it PROUDLY on that field. Ready to celebrate Christmas in August, thank you very much.

Watching her march to her own drum with zero apologies, I realized she was developing ME. Her audacity was developing my audacity. Her fearless authenticity was giving me permission to be even more myself.

Sometimes just by being that light—by shining that energy and showing up in your true bold, audacious purpose— you're literally developing other people's courage to step into theirs. *You become living proof that different is not only okay, it's powerful.*

Development isn't some stuffy formal mentoring program where you sit across from someone with a clipboard. Real development happens in those everyday moments: When you share vulnerably about your own struggles—the messy, imperfect journey of how you clawed your way through. When you celebrate someone else's tiny win with the enthusiasm of a champion. When you ask the questions that help others discover their own answers instead of just handing them yours. When you model boundary-setting that shows others they can prioritize themselves too.

THE RIPPLE EFFECT OF DEVELOPMENT

The ripple effect works because seeing is believing. When people observe you taking audacious action despite fear, they begin to consider what might be possible for them. When they watch you recover from a setback with resilience, they develop confidence in their own ability to bounce back.

I've witnessed this front row in my own family. My kids don't just listen to my speeches about pursuing goals or living authentically—they're watching every move I make. When they see me terrified but taking action anyway, they absorb that courage in their bones. Way more powerful than any "be brave" pep talk I could give them.

Sometimes I get little reminders of just how closely they're watching. One night, while I was juggling a million things—dinner, emails, dog walk, rushing Drew to a late-night baseball game—Adelyn asked for a piece of paper. The next day, I found that piece of paper folded into a note and stuffed in my laptop. In her six-year-old handwriting, Adelyn wrote words that hit me straight in the heart—love bombs reminding me she notices what I do and who I am more than I sometimes realize.

Like that note from Adelyn, what we leave behind for others isn't measured in possessions but in impact. Legacy isn't built through grand gestures or monuments to our greatness. It's built in the spaces between our accomplishments—in how we show up day after day, in who we choose to be when no one is watching, and in the values we embody rather than just espouse.

I think often about my grandparents and the invisible threads they wove that still guide me today. My maternal grandmother never set out to create a legacy. She simply lived her values with unwavering consistency. Every summer at Cape Cod, she'd put on her flippers and swim cap and swim half a mile daily, her strong strokes cutting through the Atlantic as we children watched in awe from the shore. Those were lessons in discipline, in connecting with nature, in honoring your body's strength.

My grandfather Arthur approached legacy differently but no less powerfully. A mechanical engineer by training, he taught through demonstration rather than declaration. I can still feel the smooth wood of his workbench under my small hands as he guided me through projects, his attention to detail showing me that excellence matters even when no one else will notice. He rarely spoke of values like precision, patience, or craftsmanship—he simply embodied them, allowing me to absorb these principles through proximity and practice.

My Polish grandmother, Babci, created legacy through nurture. The moment we walked through her door, she'd usher us to the kitchen where candy dishes sat filled, the refrigerator stocked with 7-Up, and Klondike bars waited in the freezer. This wasn't just about feeding us—it was about creating a space where we felt anticipated, valued, and abundantly cared for. Her legacy lives in how I welcome others into my home, in the small gestures that say "I've been looking forward to you."

What I loved most was all the way through post college, Babci would handwrite me letters—telling me everything from the weather in Massachusetts, to what trip she was taking, to how much she missed me. I would write her back.

This exchange went on for almost a decade, until her writing due to arthritis was so challenging, I could barely read the writing or understand the message. However, I still have some of those very letters today. And this is a tradition I have passed to my kids—NOTHING beats a stamp, a handwritten note, and the time someone took to show you THEY CARE. Which is one of many reasons that the note from Adelyn hit so deep.

Legacy is built through all the little things you do each and every day—like sprinkling breadcrumbs. Every interaction, every choice, every moment of presence or absence is a deposit into what you'll ultimately leave behind. The account grows not through occasional large investments but through consistent small contributions. How you make people feel, how you navigate challenges, how you celebrate successes, how you recover from failures—these daily deposits compound over time into something far more valuable than any material inheritance.

The most powerful truth about legacy is that you're creating it right now, whether intentionally or not. The question isn't whether you'll leave a legacy—it's what kind of legacy you're building with each passing day.

The essence of real connection and development doesn't happen through speeches or soapboxes. It happens through presence. Through modeling. Through showing up authentically—messy and brave and human—and letting people see what's possible and that you care.

True development meets people where they are. Not everyone is ready for the same level of expansion. Some people are taking their first baby steps away from playing small. Others are ready to take a flying leap off the cliff of comfort. Honor these differences, and you create space where everyone can grow at their own pace.

The best development flows both ways. Even as you're helping others expand, stay open to what they can teach you. Some of my most life-changing lessons came from people I was supposedly mentoring. This reciprocity creates a dynamic flow of growth that lifts everyone up.

And for the love of all things good—celebrate the wins! Recognize and acknowledge growth, both yours and others', to reinforce this expansion journey. When we mark milestones and victories, we create evidence that feeds belief, which fuels even more development.

PUTTING BOLD ALL TOGETHER

As powerful as development is on its own, it reaches its full potential when integrated with the other elements of BOLD. While each component serves a vital purpose individually, their true power emerges when they function as an integrated system—creating a synergy that transforms personal growth into lasting impact.

When belief and ownership combine, they create a self-reinforcing loop of confidence that builds exponential momentum. Each action you take and fully own creates tangible evidence that reinforces your belief in what's possible. That strengthened belief, in turn, fuels greater commitment to your daily process.

Owning your process doesn't mean following someone else's blueprint—it means taking responsibility for designing systems that work with your authentic self, not against it. When you build consistency around who you actually are rather than who you think you should be, you create a framework sturdy enough to withstand the inevitable storms of setbacks and uncertainty. This authentic ownership, paired with strategic support from others, becomes the foundation for sustainable expansion.

When you simultaneously receive support and develop others, you create reciprocal growth relationships that amplify impact beyond what any individual could achieve alone. The guidance you receive doesn't simply benefit you—it transforms through your unique perspective and gets paid forward, creating overlapping cycles of development.

As you develop others, you witness transformations that would have seemed impossible at the outset. These tangible changes reinforce your belief in both the development process and in human potential itself. This strengthened belief then makes you a more effective developer, creating a self-reinforcing loop of impact.

Understanding these integration points conceptually is helpful, but seeing the BOLD method applied to real challenges makes it truly actionable. Let's use fear as an example—one of the most common barriers to expansion.

Imagine you've been working in accounting for ten years but have always dreamed of starting your own consulting business. The idea excites you, but it also terrifies you. Here's how the integrated BOLD method transforms your response:

Believe: Instead of fixating on all the ways it could fail, you deliberately review your evidence. You recall the time you helped your neighbor organize her small business finances and she increased her profit by 30%. You remember the colleagues who've asked for your advice on financial planning. You acknowledge the specific feedback you've received about your ability to explain complex concepts in simple terms.

Own: Rather than becoming paralyzed by the enormity of "starting a business," you break the challenge into manageable steps that leverage your natural strengths and work style. You recognize that your methodical, detail-oriented nature (what you once saw as "boring") is actually perfect for thorough market research, so you schedule focused research sessions this week. You acknowledge that your ability to simplify complex financial concepts—something colleagues always come to you for—is your unique value proposition, so you build your business plan around that strength by month's end. Instead of forcing yourself into aggressive sales tactics that feel inauthentic, you leverage your natural relationship-building style by reaching out to five potential clients within 30 days through genuine conversations about their challenges.

Lean: You connect with your former professor who runs a successful consulting firm for guidance on pricing strategies. You ask your most entrepreneurial friend to be your accountability partner. You join a local small business networking group where you can learn from others who've made similar transitions.

Develop: You start documenting your transition journey on LinkedIn, sharing both the exciting moments and the challenging ones. A coworker mentions she's also considering a career change, so you share your research process and introduce her to the networking group you joined.

This integrated approach creates forward momentum that no amount of motivational quotes or positive thinking alone could generate. The power lies in the harmonious interaction of all four elements working together, each amplifying the others to create a whole greater than the sum of its parts.

Translating the BOLD method from concept to daily practice requires intentionality and structure. Begin by pinpointing where you're ready to grow beyond your current boundaries. This edge isn't about making superficial changes—it's about identifying areas where expansion would create meaningful impact in your life and the lives of others.

Ask yourself these revealing questions: What area of life feels ripe for breakthrough? What would I pursue if fear wasn't a factor in my decision-making? What's the true cost of remaining in my current comfort zone? What recurring thought keeps nudging me toward change?

Once you've identified your expansion edge, apply all four components of BOLD in a coordinated approach. Create a specific evidence list for this particular challenge. Define three micro-steps you'll take in the next seventy-two hours. Identify two to three specific people who can provide the support you need. Determine how you'll document and share your journey to help others who might face similar challenges.

When we integrate the BOLD framework with authenticity, we create powerful ripple effects that extend far beyond our individual growth. Research consistently shows that organizations with authentic leadership see significantly higher employee trust, innovation, and retention. The psychological safety that stems from seeing leaders integrate their authentic selves with professional excellence creates environments where expansion becomes the norm rather than the exception.

As leaders, we have a unique opportunity to catalyze expansion by creating spaces where authenticity is valued as a strategic asset rather than a vulnerability to be hidden. This requires consistent modeling of integrated expansion through daily practices, brave conversations that challenge comfortable norms, and actively creating opportunities for others to practice BOLD integration in their own lives.

We weren't put here to play small. We were put here to leave that legacy. To leave the best footprints, the best confetti, the best sprinkles of glitter on this universe, to be able to make a legacy, to make a difference, to make a change.

The most audacious act might be recognizing that your growth was never just about you. Every step you take toward your potential creates a pathway for others to follow. Every fear you face with courage gives someone else permission to be brave. Every authentic choice you make expands what's possible for everyone around you.

AUDACITY IN ACTION CHALLENGE

This week, practice integrated BOLD development: Identify your current expansion edge—one area where you're ready to grow beyond your comfort zone. Apply the BOLD framework systematically:

Believe: Create an evidence list specific to this challenge.

Own: Break it into three concrete actions you'll take this week that fit your unique qualities.

Lean: Reach out to one person who can support this growth.

Develop: Share your process with someone who could benefit from your journey. Document the ripple effects you notice when you integrate all four elements rather than focusing on just one.

SHARE YOUR JOURNEY

⊛ "Using the BOLD method to turn my expansion into legacy. What ripple effects are you creating? #AudaciousExpansion"

Part 4:

EXPANDING INTO ACTION

Don't forget to download your free journal before continuing.

Chapter 16

PLANS WITH SWAGGER

Small, consistent investments yield remarkable returns over time.

How many times have you thought, "I just need to get through this one thing, then everything will be fine"?

(Raises hand frantically.)

I used to think that way too. After my assault, I believed if I could just get through the trial, everything would be okay. During marathon training, I thought if I could just finish that one race, I'd feel accomplished. In my corporate life, I convinced myself that if I could just get that next promotion or that corner office, I'd finally feel successful.

But growth isn't about reaching some magical finish line where you suddenly become a fully actualized human being who has it all figured out. (If you find that place, please send me the GPS coordinates.)

It's about embracing the beautiful, messy marathon of life—one ridiculous mile marker at a time—and being *in the moment.*

We live in a world where everything comes with a "Prime" label. Two-day shipping, on-demand everything, instant downloads, quick-fix solutions, and those "I became a millionaire overnight" stories that flood your Instagram feed. But real transformation—genuine, lasting change—doesn't work that way. As Arianna Huffington reminds us, "Resilience is an on-demand quality we cannot do without—a constant process rather than a destination. Not a marker to reach, but a mindset."[1]

Think about the last time you achieved something significant. Was it really about that final champagne-popping moment? Or was it about the unglamorous 5 AM alarms, the quiet dedication when nobody was watching, the days when you questioned everything but showed up anyway?

Success isn't built in the spotlight moments—it's forged in the shadows, where the real work happens and nobody's taking pictures for social media.

I saw this principle in action with my daughter's Girls on the Run program. On day one, Adelyn could barely make it around the school once. But by showing up twice a week for twelve weeks, she crossed the finish line of a 5K—smiling, strong, and unstoppable.

Steady, consistent action is the key (are you noticing a pattern here?). I've shared this same principle with construction foremen—tough, practical men who pride themselves on physical results. I introduced them to Mark Breslin's concept from *The 5 Minute Foreman*: that investing just five intentional minutes each day in leadership—thinking, reflecting, connecting—adds up to 20 full hours over the course of a year.[2]

When I asked if they would dedicate a full workweek to personal development, most said absolutely not—too busy, too much lost income. But five minutes daily? That felt doable. What if they doubled it to ten minutes? That's 40 hours yearly—a full workweek of development that doesn't disrupt their lives but transforms them gradually. This is the magic of compound interest applied to personal growth. Small, consistent investments yield remarkable returns over time.

This goes for anything you choose you want to accomplish.

THE IGNITION EFFECT

They say the heaviest weight at the gym is the front door. Starting is always the hardest part. Think about a car ignition—the moment when everything shifts from stillness to momentum. Getting that initial momentum requires significant power. Once the car is moving, maintaining speed takes far less energy. Our expansion works the same way.

Building new habits feels extraordinarily difficult at first. Every fiber of your being resists change. But once those habits become part of your daily rhythm, maintaining them requires much less willpower.

The challenge with expansion is that it isn't sustainable when it relies solely on motivation. Motivation fluctuates daily; some mornings you'll bound out of bed ready to conquer the world, and other days you'll struggle to find the energy to start. That's why sustainable success requires systems—reliable frameworks that carry you forward even when motivation wanes.

The difference between goals and systems is crucial here. Goals are the destinations; systems are the vehicles that get you there. Goals provide direction, but systems create results. Research suggests it takes approximately 66 days to form a sustainable habit—far longer than the common myth of 21 days. This means you need to prepare for the long game, creating systems that can weather the inevitable dips in motivation.

I've found certain principles crucial to building sustainable daily disciplines:

Start with the hard things. It's easy to knock off simple tasks just for the satisfaction of checking boxes. I've been guilty of writing down things I've already done just to check them off! But real expansion comes from tackling the difficult, uncomfortable work first—when your energy and resolve are highest.

Defend your time fiercely. Some of us are juggling careers, caregiving, side hustles, and personal healing. Life throws different demands at each of us. How we choose to use our time—even in small, intentional ways—defines what we're building. I'm not saying hustle harder. I'm saying get radically honest about what matters most to you—and then fiercely protect the time it takes to build it.

Track your progress meticulously. What gets measured gets managed. When I wanted to read more books, I created a tracking system on my whiteboard. My daughter Adelyn would come into my office and ask, "Mommy, have you finished any books? Can I write another one down?" That simple accountability system helped me read 18 books last year instead of my goal of 12—and I'm on track for even more this year.

To build sustainable systems, start ridiculously small. Don't begin with one hour of daily meditation if you've never meditated before. Start with one minute. Make the barrier to entry so low that you can't talk yourself out of it. Then, stack new habits onto existing ones. If you already make coffee every morning, use that time to review your daily priorities or practice gratitude. Remove as much friction as possible—set out your workout clothes the night before, keep your journal and pen on your nightstand, prepare healthy meals in advance. Make the path of least resistance the one that leads to your expansion.

Jim Collins, in his book *Good to Great*, introduces the concept of the flywheel—a massive, heavy disk mounted on an axle. Getting it to move initially requires tremendous effort. You push and push, making what feels like minimal progress.

But each push adds a little more momentum. Eventually, the flywheel begins to move on its own, and your job shifts from initiating movement to simply maintaining it.[3]

Your expansion works the same way. Those first steps—those first weeks of new habits, those initial awkward attempts at a new skill—require immense effort for seemingly little reward. But each consistent action adds momentum. Eventually, your expansion creates its own energy. Reading becomes a craving rather than a chore. Exercise becomes something you miss if you skip it. Your authentic self begins to emerge naturally rather than requiring conscious effort. This is when expansion becomes truly powerful—when it shifts from something you're pushing yourself to do to something that pulls you forward.

Often, to expand, we need to change our mindset first. The stories we tell ourselves daily shape what we believe is possible. It's easy to look at others who have achieved what we want and assume they have advantages we don't—more time, more money, more support, more talent. We scroll through social media seeing people who seem far ahead of us, forgetting the uphill battles they faced to get there. We sometimes forget what they've been through and focus only on our own battle wounds, our own scars, making excuses for why we can't be where we want to be.

The differentiating factor between those who expand and those who remain stuck isn't circumstances—it's the decision to keep moving forward despite circumstances. It's using pain as purpose. It's getting up each day knowing you are capable of something absolutely magnificent.

Is it easy? Hell no. But when you allow yourself to change your mindset, to fully expand into the best version of yourself, that's when things start unlocking. It doesn't mean you won't have setbacks or that every day will be a magical fairy tale. It does mean that every day you're growing, evolving, and changing. Imagine if every day you woke up just a little bit more positive, with a better mindset, with the ability to say: "Today, I am willing to expand. Today, I am willing to change. Today, I am willing to open doors I once never knew existed."

You weren't made to blend in—you were made to break the mold. Stop shrinking to fit spaces that were never meant to hold your brilliance. Your expectations shape your reality more than your circumstances ever could, and confidence bends that reality in your favor. Energy doesn't lie—you attract what you radiate. Focus on what's meant for you, and watch it expand. The moment you stop underestimating your worth is the moment everything begins to shift.

Once you build momentum, your expansion will take on a life of its own.

AUDACITY IN ACTION CHALLENGE

This week, implement strategic action planning:

Create One Tracking System: Choose one habit that supports your expansion and design a visible tracking system. Place it somewhere you'll see daily and enlist an accountability partner who will check in on your progress regularly.

Identify Your Resistance Points: List the three most common reasons you abandon consistent action (such as time, money, fear, etc). For each resistance point, create a specific "if-then" plan to overcome it when it inevitably arises.

SHARE YOUR JOURNEY

✺ "I'm building strategic systems for expansion by tracking one key habit and preparing for my resistance points so that consistency becomes my superpower. What system are you putting in place to support your growth? #AudaciousExpansion"

Chapter 17:

FUEL UP ON FEAR

We become the story we choose to believe.

I started wearing a weighted vest during my workouts and walks this year. (P.S. For my fellow women reading this: there are some incredible benefits worth knowing about with weighted vest training. It helps build bone density (hello, protection against osteoporosis!), improves posture and core strength, and can actually boost our metabolism more effectively than traditional cardio alone. #addweight) At first, it felt awkward—yes, I even wore the vest upside down a few times!

The weighted vest became my metaphor for facing fears. Some days, the added pressure felt overwhelming, and I needed to take it off to rest. Other days, I pushed harder, adding just enough resistance to reach new heights. Growth comes from knowing when to challenge yourself and when to let go. That's where transformation truly lives.

Fear operates much the same way. It can either become a weight that crushes us or one that strengthens us—the difference lies in how we choose to carry it.

Fear is one of the most powerful forces that can paralyze us. Fear creates chains that prevent us from growing. It starts a war in our heads, telling stories about why we can't or shouldn't move forward: *There's not enough money. There's not enough time. There's not enough space. We're too late. We're too early. We missed the boat. We're not worthy.*

These narratives loop in our minds, especially the fear that we're simply not enough. And here's the truth—I don't care how much money you have in your bank account, what status you've achieved, or who you are—everyone experiences these fears. They strike at different levels and at different times in our lives.

I know this because fear creeps into my life too. No matter what manifestation I wrote that morning or what inspiring book I read, fear still sneaks in. Sometimes the negative thoughts ooze into my consciousness, and even when I know they sound crazy, they continue dominating my mind. Here's what's wild—commonly cited figures show the average person has somewhere between 12,000 and 60,000 thoughts per day and about 80% of them are negative. As if that's not bad enough, 95% are the same thoughts on repeat.[1] That's a staggering amount of brain power dedicated to what could go wrong, what we're not good enough for, and why we should stay small and safe.

I remember countless nights filled with fear after my attack, lying in bed terrified that my attacker, even though I knew he was in a correctional facility, would somehow appear at my front door. The fear felt so real, so overwhelming. I don't think we should try to make fear disappear with a snap of our fingers—if only it were that easy! Instead, we must acknowledge that the biggest fear often exists only in our own minds.

When we feel fear rising, it's usually resistance. I believe it's often the universe challenging us, testing whether we're ready for what's coming. However, our modern world is primed to panic—so much so that networks like CNN have overused "Breaking News" to the point where its urgency is nearly meaningless, prompting leadership to cut back on the frequency.[2]

But more often than not, our fears are just stories—narratives in our heads about what might happen. In fact, research shows that about 91% of our fears don't come true.[3] Just sit with that for a moment. All the late-night spirals, the "what ifs" that steal our peace, the scenarios we play over and over in our minds—almost all of them vanish into nothing. And even in the rare cases where our fears do unfold, they're usually not as devastating as we imagined.

Fear wants to keep us small. But the truth? We're stronger than our worst-case scenarios.

When we push through fear and resistance to serve others, we often find our greatest purpose. Consider resistance a signal that you're moving in the right direction. When you feel that fear rising, ask yourself: What if this isn't a warning to stop but an invitation to continue?

But, I want to pause here briefly to make sure I'm being clear on this—and this is critical—leaning into fear isn't always the audacious choice. Sometimes the most audacious decision is recognizing when NOT to lean into a particular fear. Sometimes wisdom means going around it, mitigating it, or choosing a different path entirely. Just like audacious expansion doesn't always mean big, bold, and brave, audacious fear management doesn't always mean charging straight ahead.

When facing a decision that scares you, ask yourself these questions: What's the worst that could happen? Could I recover from this worst-case scenario? What's the best that could happen? What happens if I do nothing? As author H. Jackson Brown Jr. once wrote (in a line often attributed to Mark Twain), "Twenty years from now, you will be more disappointed by the things you didn't do than by the ones you did do."[4]

The truth is, even when you push through the fear and take action, you're still going to fail sometimes. Not because you didn't believe enough or work hard enough, but because failure is simply part of the expansion process.

Andy and I once decided to open a gym. We partnered with another couple on a new location, investing our time, sweat, tears, and equity into the venture. The plan was for us to be financial investors and help with setup while our partners handled daily operations.

About eighteen months after opening, we decided to close it. I felt shameful and upset with ourselves. Looking back, I realized we hadn't taken enough time to investigate the risks, rewards, and the partnership we were building.

We thought we had dotted all our I's and crossed all our T's, but like many things in life, we acted partly out of excitement and gut instincts. That's how I tend to operate—fortunately, my husband is the one who works through the nuances, what-ifs, and calculations. Even so, sometimes you still make the wrong decision.

While we lost significant time, money, effort, energy, and experienced frustration, we don't regret taking the risk. At the end of the day, if those risks won't prevent you from putting food on the table or impact your safety, all you're risking is energy and money—things that can be recovered.

Could we have taken a better calculated risk? Perhaps. But I firmly believe you need to trust your intuition. Your gut won't always be one hundred percent right—failures and setbacks will happen. If we take the time to evaluate every risk, every chance, every what-if, we probably won't do anything at all—we'll just maintain the status quo because change feels unsafe and uneasy.

Look at any successful entrepreneur—they've likely failed many times. Sara Blakely cut the feet off her pantyhose, pitched her idea to countless manufacturers who said no, and got rejected by department stores before Spanx became a billion-dollar empire. Oprah was fired from her first television job and told she was "unfit for television news." But they kept showing up, kept refining their vision, kept pushing through the rejection.

Taking calculated risks doesn't mean blindly jumping into every opportunity. It means weighing the potential outcomes, understanding what you can afford to lose, and making deliberate choices that align with your values and goals.

Sometimes we know our own risks, our own resistance, and when we're actually ready. We need to listen to that intuition. Sometimes it leads to the right decision, sometimes what you may call the wrong one. But at least we're making a decision and growing from the lessons we're meant to learn.

Inaction can be one of the worst places to be. More often than not, when we don't act on our gut feelings, we end up with regret.

Forward motion doesn't mean you'll never falter or fall. It means that when you do—because everyone does at some point—you find the strength to get back up and keep moving. Sometimes, rest is an active and necessary decision—taking time to regroup, reassess, and recharge. But do not set up camp there indefinitely. Each step forward, no matter how small, is progress.

Pain will push us until purpose decides to drive us. It's about deciding how we want to navigate that pain and what we want it to feel like as we work through it. When we have a clear sense of purpose, it can help us transform pain into fuel for growth and resilience.

We're all destined to do extraordinary things, but 95% of life won't go as planned. Only about 5% goes right, and that's what stops many people—most days are harder than they are easy.

But when we stop making excuses, when we refuse to stay stuck, when we become mission-minded and recognize we have a legacy to leave—not just the legacy we leave when we depart this earth, but the legacy we live every day—that's when expansion happens.

This expansion requires us to prioritize our peace and well-being. As Trent Shelton emphasizes, protecting your peace is crucial—the idea that your mental and emotional well-being is sacred territory that deserves fierce protection.[5] Whenever you feel yourself reacting to something that doesn't deserve your energy, pause and remind yourself: "My peace is more important."

Choosing peace over proving a point, and calm over chaos, isn't a sign of weakness—it's a strategic decision. It's something I teach, speak, and live by in every keynote and training room: We can't control others; we can only control how we respond. Taking that pause before you react is critical when you're operating from a place of fear.

The key to carrying any weight—whether a physical weighted vest or the challenges of an audacious goal—is staying laser-focused on why you're carrying it in the first place. When fear creeps in, reconnect with your purpose. What drives you? Who are you serving? What legacy are you creating?

Creating practices that help you manage your fear response—deep breathing, journaling, speaking affirmations, physical movement, talking with trusted advisors—allows you to make decisions from a place of clarity rather than fear.

Facing our fears head-on is a crucial part of this process. Just like a kid learning to ride a bike, we could stay on training wheels forever, safe and stable, but we'll never experience the freedom of truly riding.

Remember that this doesn't mean we should always charge blindly into our fears. The art lies in discernment—knowing when to lean in and when to step back, when to push through and when to pivot, when to face the fear head-on and when to find another route that still gets you where you need to go. It's choosing to make decisions that serve your bigger purpose—being led by intention, not fear.

Our energy is contagious—both good and bad. Choose to spread the energy of courage rather than fear. How many times have you stayed stuck in fear instead of plowing through it? Start consciously choosing a narrative of courage, resilience, and possibility. Fear will always be present when you're pursuing audacious goals. Will you let it stop you, or will you use it as fuel?

The most extraordinary achievements in your life will require you to do things that scare you. Your fear is the gateway to your greatest growth.

EXPANSION IN ACTION CHALLENGE

This week, practice breaking through fear with these three steps:

1. **Fear Inventory:** Take 20 minutes to list every fear currently holding you back from expansion. Next to each fear, write what you'd do if that fear wasn't present. Choose the one fear that's limiting you most and commit to taking one small action to move through it this week.

2. **Resilience Reminder:** Create a visual reminder of your resilience, such as a post-it note or phone background with a phrase like "I am stronger than my fears" or "I breathe through resistance." Place this reminder in a prominent location where you'll see it daily, and use it as a prompt to reconnect with your inner strength when fear arises.

3. **Calculated Risk Assessment:** Identify one audacious goal currently paralyzed by fear. Complete a risk analysis by answering: What's the worst that could happen? Could I recover from it? What's the best that could happen? What happens if I do nothing? Based on your answers, determine one forward action you can take within 48 hours.

SHARE YOUR JOURNEY

✸ "I'm turning fear into fuel by reminding myself of my resilience every day. I'm taking calculated risks and moving forward despite resistance. How are you breaking through fear to live more audaciously? #AudaciousExpansion"'

Chapter 18:

HELL YES OR HARD NO

Stop taking advice from people you wouldn't switch lives with.

When I hear people say, "You've changed," I say, "Yes, I have."

I've been more honest with myself.

I've been saying "no" more.

I've stopped chasing and forcing things.

I've been committed to my purpose and passions.

I've stopped worrying about what other people think (within reason).

I've been more selective with my time and energy.

I've been listening more to my heart and soul.

I've been more myself than ever—and it feels so good.

Creating boundaries has never been an easy place for me to be. There's that constant desire to say yes to everything, to please everyone, and I think especially for many women, we hesitate to establish clear boundaries. We want to be everything to everybody. Setting those lanes, trying not to cross over, not wanting life to get messy—these are challenging aspects of boundary-setting that I've struggled with for years.

But the older I get, the more I realize I need to protect my own boundaries—boundaries of energy, boundaries against toxic relationships, boundaries for inner peace, and boundaries that allow me to be true to myself. I'd be lying if I said I've mastered this art or figured it out perfectly. Sometimes my boundaries get really blurred, and other times they're crystal clear.

Many times, I push those limits and boundaries. And at the end of the day, when I reflect on times I've pushed beyond my boundaries, those are the moments I end up regretting. Those are the times I wish I hadn't pushed so hard because I end up feeling depleted, frustrated, anxious, and upset with myself.

I realized this in my relationship with my father. I wanted so badly to have the relationship that looked perfect from the outside—to have that dad I could call with any problem or issue. The dad I was yearning for was never going to be that person. I don't necessarily want to blame him; he likely experienced things I'll never know about. But there have been so many issues over the years, so many times I've actually tried to cut him out of my life completely and then gone back. What I realized is that sometimes going back and forth and floundering, instead of just deciding what lane I needed to be in for my own emotional health, kept me in this exhausting cycle. I was always making myself feel guilty that I wasn't giving him enough or wasn't being a good enough daughter, and that's been challenging, even as an adult.

But after working through a lot of therapy over many years and stopping my attempts to build a fairy tale, I recognized I needed to establish boundaries—boundaries around how much time, effort, and energy I'd invest in a relationship that wasn't meeting my needs.

I was looking for something that wasn't necessarily there. Once I started establishing boundaries, once I stopped feeling guilty for having expectations that weren't being met, something shifted. The best lesson I've learned as I've gotten older is that the only person I can control is myself. Not the person to my right or left, not when I'll get the job or promotion, not when I'll land the new gig. It's always about deciding how I want to show up because that's the only portion I can control.

THE WORK OF BOUNDARIES

There were so many years when I didn't have healthy boundaries, especially at work. I would say yes to everything. I thought I had to be that people pleaser. I wanted everyone to like me, thinking that if I agreed to everything—from coordinating barbecues for employee appreciation day to preparing perfect project performance reviews for management meetings to being on site two or three times a week while still trying to be a mom and wife—people would respect me more. (And I am still guilty of this... it's damn hard work.)

What I realized is that the only person I was fooling was myself—fooling myself by not establishing those boundaries, by not giving myself the time and energy to be where I truly needed to be, in the lanes that would allow me to function at my best. All too often, our boundaries start out strong but gradually weaken.

This was a life-changing shift for me. Years ago, when people criticized me, I let it land. I gave equal weight to every opinion without stopping to consider the context, intent, or credibility behind it. Then I came across one powerful truth that flipped everything: Stop taking advice from people you wouldn't switch lives with. Read that again. Let it sink in. Before you absorb criticism, ask yourself, would I trade lives with this person? If the answer is no, why let their words shape your world? Next time someone tries to invalidate you, consider the context, consider the source.

As we discussed, one of the most powerful lessons I've learned is that "no" is a complete sentence. It's about recognizing your limits and honoring your needs, even when it feels uncomfortable. The guilt that often follows boundary-setting is a liar whispering that you're selfish or unkind. In reality, you are not responsible for other people's reactions to your boundaries.

When I've implemented these principles through strategic "no's," I've discovered I have more energy for the things that truly matter. Instead of spreading myself thin across numerous commitments, I can channel my focus into the areas where I'll have the greatest impact. This is wise stewardship of the limited resources we all have: time, energy, and attention.

As Mel Robbins explains in her now-viral *Let Them Theory*, the key to peace is simple: stop trying to control other people. "If your friends aren't inviting you out to brunch this weekend—let them. If the person you're really into doesn't want a commitment—let them. If your kids don't feel like going to that thing with you this week—let them. So much time and energy is wasted trying to force other people to meet our expectations."[1] If someone you're dating, working with, or loving isn't showing up the way you need them to, don't waste your life trying to make them change. Let them be who they are. Because in doing that, they're showing you exactly what's true—and then you get to decide what to do next.

The boundaries we create actually serve as expansion tools rather than limitations. They create the container within which we can grow most effectively. Just like a plant needs the right-sized pot to flourish—too small and its growth is stunted, too large and its energy is scattered—we need appropriately defined boundaries to channel our energy effectively.

When we don't have healthy boundaries, our energy disperses in too many directions. We may find ourselves constantly exhausted, resentful, or unable to focus on what truly matters. By creating intentional space through boundaries, we reclaim our power to choose what deserves our precious time and attention.

Setting boundaries is actually an act of love—both for yourself and others. It recognizes your worth and prioritizes your emotional health. Ironically, it can also be an act of love for others, as it creates healthier relationship dynamics and prevents resentment from building. Boundaries help create sustainable connections rather than exhausting yourself to maintain appearances.

When we make choices aligned with our true selves, we create a ripple effect of authenticity in all our relationships. Making aligned choices means you're no longer living to please others but to honor your authentic self. You can rise up from anything. You can completely recreate yourself. Nothing is permanent. You're not stuck. You have choices. You can think new thoughts. You can learn something new. You can create new habits. All that matters is that you decide today and never look back.

By clearing your life of energy-draining relationships and commitments, you make room for new growth, new opportunities, and new ways of being. When you create space by setting boundaries, that space doesn't stay empty for long. It fills with possibilities more aligned with your authentic self.

Think about your own life right now. What are your boundaries? What boundaries are you putting in place to protect the things that are most important to you? What are you saying no to so you can say yes to other things?

What boundaries do you need to defend better? It's easy to be manipulated. It's easy to feel like you need to do it all. But once you start establishing those boundaries, you build a shield—you build your armor and say no to things that don't serve you, which is incredibly liberating. It actually allows you to flow and exist in a space where you don't feel controlled by others, where you're not doing things you don't want to do or trying to be in eighteen different places at once because you didn't honor your own limits.

Within those boundaries, it's essential to ensure that you're operating as your highest self with the best potential. This means being intentional about the commitments you make and the relationships you cultivate. It involves regularly checking in with yourself to assess whether your actions and decisions align with your values and goals. When we allow others to cross our boundaries or when we don't respect our own limits, we can't give our best in any aspect of life.

Ultimately, boundaries are about recognizing your worth and fighting for your emotional well-being. It's about prioritizing your needs, setting healthy limits, and knowing when to let go of relationships or commitments that no longer serve you. It's about self-advocacy and self-love.

You are worth fighting for. And the next time someone says, "You've changed," remember that it might be the greatest compliment they could give you.

EXPANSION IN ACTION CHALLENGE

This week, strengthen your boundaries as expansion tools with these two steps:

1. **Boundary Audit:** Take inventory of where your current boundaries are strong and where they're weak or non-existent. Identify the three areas where poor boundaries are most depleting your energy. For each

area, define one clear, specific boundary you'll establish this week (e.g., "I will not check email after 7 PM" or "I will decline meetings that don't include an agenda").

2. **Strategic No Practice:** Commit to saying "no" to two requests this week that don't align with your highest priorities. Before each refusal, pause to create a response that is kind but firm. Remember that "no" doesn't require explanation, but if you choose to provide one, keep it brief and don't apologize for honoring your boundaries.

3. **Relationship Boundary Reset:** Identify one relationship where you consistently give more energy than you receive or where your boundaries are regularly crossed. This week, have one honest conversation about your needs or implement one specific boundary change. This might mean limiting contact with an energy vampire, asking for reciprocal support from someone who only takes, or clearly communicating your availability limits to someone who assumes unlimited access to your time.

SHARE YOUR JOURNEY

✴ "I'm redefining my boundaries this week by saying 'no' to what doesn't align with my core purpose so I can say 'YES' to what truly matters. Boundaries aren't walls—they're windows to our most expansive selves. What boundary are you strengthening today? #AudaciousExpansion"

Chapter 19:

BOUNCE BACK LIKE A BOSS

You were never meant to shrink. You were meant to rise.

Life is a lot like a rubber band. We're often tempted to stay in that familiar, comfortable place—stretched just enough to function, but never so far that we risk snapping. We move back and forth between progress and comfort, afraid that if we stretch too much, we'll break. But what if the real danger isn't in stretching too far—it's in never stretching enough?

Think about it. How many times have you settled for "almost"—almost taking the leap, almost pursuing the dream, almost stepping into the next version of yourself—only to retreat back to the safety of what you know? It's natural. We are wired for comfort. Even before we entered the world, we started in the ultimate comfort zone: the womb. Cushioned, warm, safe. And yet, at some point, we had no choice but to leave that space and enter a world that demanded we grow, adapt, and expand—crying, screaming, and uncertain.

Research shows that when we experience failure or social rejection, the brain's stress system releases cortisol, pulling us out of feelings of safety.[1] By contrast, rewarding experiences trigger dopamine and other "feel-good" chemicals that reinforce the behaviors that led to success.[2] As neuroscientist Lisa Feldman Barrett explains, the brain's primary job isn't to make us happy or successful—it's to keep the body alive.[3] This survival-first programming means your brain will often choose the familiar discomfort of staying stuck over the uncertain territory of growth, even when that growth could transform your entire life.

Expansion is not new to you. You've done it before—in fact, you were built for it. Think about the hardest moments of your life—the gut punches you never saw coming. Losing someone you loved. Getting the diagnosis you feared. Facing the job loss you didn't expect. Being forced into change you weren't ready for. You didn't plan to expand then. *But you did expand.* You grew resilience, you deepened your courage, you found strength you never knew you had.

FINDING YOUR AUTHENTIC PATH

The truth is, most of us only stretch when life demands it. But what if this time, you stretched because you chose to? What if you decided to expand not because of crisis, but because of calling? Not out of desperation, but out of determination?

Just like Roger Bannister, who shattered the belief that no human could run a mile in under four minutes—and in doing so, unlocked the potential in hundreds of runners who came after him—you too can break your own internal barriers. You too can challenge what's possible, first in your mind, then in your reality.

My mom would frequently say, "I always want to give you roots, but I also want to give you wings." The quote is a reminder that we can always root back to what feels comfortable, but if we never expand our wings, if we're never willing to fly, if we're never willing to take the chance and do the things that seem scary, then are we really living?

I don't know what your expansions have been, but I can guarantee that you've had them. So go back, take the time to remind yourself: Where have you made that expansion already? Because *you are already audacious*, even if you've never associated yourself with that word before. Sometimes we forget all of those steps that we took because looking back, we forget that they were leaps of faith in the moment. We forget that we felt nervous, and we felt scared.

For me, I chose to stay rooted many times in my life, chose to stay really comfortable because it seemed easier than expanding those wings. But every time I've opened those wings—perhaps it was when I decided to go to college and move three hundred miles away from home, perhaps it was when I decided to first lace up those boots and go onto that construction site, perhaps it was the time I decided to leave an ex-boyfriend who I thought was going to be the man I married, realizing that he really wasn't the person I was supposed to live the rest of my life with—I grew.

Once you start thinking about those expansion moments, they'll keep rolling for you like they did for me. Deciding to move to Pennsylvania and take that leap of faith for that new job. Deciding to backpack Europe for six weeks after college. Choosing to go for my MBA while working fulltime. Deciding to write this book while launching my Audacious Summit.

And then there was starting Grit, Grace and Glitz—my podcast that began as a COVID project when I felt completely disconnected from the world. I wasn't networking with anyone because the world was in a strange place—no one knew what to do. I couldn't see anyone in person. It was a tough time for me, being the type of person who thrives on being around people. So I decided to take a chance, with no idea that it would turn into something so much more than I ever imagined. What started as a simple podcast has now grown to almost 200 episodes, but more importantly, it's created connections with so many incredible people.

I specifically named it Grit, Grace and Glitz because I truly believe that sometimes we need to be audacious, gritty, and willing to expand. But that middle word—grace— is really the connection. It's the bridge that reminds us that every time we're being gritty, sometimes we have to give

GRIT GRACE & GLITZ PODCAST

ourselves grace. Sometimes we have to take that step back. Sometimes we have to say no. Sometimes we have to take that pause and remind ourselves to not only give ourselves that grace, but to give other people grace too. And on the other side, we can't forget to celebrate that glitz—the joy, the everyday victories, the impact we're making on people's lives, the things we're changing and growing.

These three elements—grit, grace, and glitz—are also essential components of authentic leadership. Leadership isn't just about corner offices or managing teams. Leadership is influence, and we're all influencing someone. Whether you're raising kids, mentoring a colleague, or simply living your values out loud, you're leading. Never question *if* you're a leader; rather, review your leadership opportunities to make sure you're leading authentically and using your influence to make a positive impact.

When we talk about authentic leadership in a corporate environment, I've always been a little bit nervous to be in that space, perhaps because I'm in an industry where less than ten percent are women. It's typically—I don't know how to say this politically correctly—but like a white boys' network. It is old school. And I know that I stand out. But sometimes I think I stand out too much.

For well over a decade, I stayed in the safe space of operations and project management, believing it was the "right" path to climb the corporate ladder. But deep down, I knew I had something unique to offer our industry—a different perspective that could make a real impact.

However, fear held me back from raising my hand and stepping into my authentic leadership. I worried that people would question my expertise because I didn't have the traditional background. Would they think I was disengaged or that I didn't belong in the network anymore? Let's face it—I never held the shovel or knew the most about gas lines and power systems. But I sensed there was another way I could contribute.

Then my boss, Jim Duffy, saw something in me that I couldn't see in myself. Jim has always been someone who sees the best in people, and when he started a new department called Performance Systems, he tapped me on the shoulder. He recognized that while I had the civil engineering degree and operational background, I could offer something more—a human element that our field desperately needed.

That position became my perfect fit. Today, I travel the country training blue-collar workers who've spent decades focused purely on the technical side of construction. I teach them to embrace the soft skills our industry rarely discusses: empathy, authentic leadership, conflict resolution, active listening, and taking ownership not just of projects, but of their own growth.

When I finally found the courage to show up authentically, my transformation was profound. Now, I bring my full personality to training sessions, sometimes even wearing bright pink pants in rooms full of hard hats and work boots. By refusing to hide who I am, I've started making a real impact. And in doing so, I've given others permission to embrace their own authenticity.

So, I want to challenge you: What would it look like if you brought your best version to every aspect of your life—work, family, friendships, and community? What if you pursued your passions and side hustles without fear of judgment? The rulebook has changed, and it's our job to break the molds and show future generations that it's okay to step into the best version of yourself.

Don't wait until you're gone to be a legacy. Start living as the legacy you want to leave behind. Embrace the things that give you a pep in your step, even if they feel uncomfortable at first.

Before we end this chapter, I want to remind you that *your expansion is a story.* It continues to change. It continues to need to be worked on. To me, there's no ending to this story. This story is a constant evolution.

There's no rush to get to the end of this book or the end of your story. When you're expanding audaciously and constantly working on growth, it's amazing what becomes possible. How you can grow. How you can push that envelope. The most expansive version of ourselves is the one that leaves the world better than we found it.

Every day presents new opportunities to step into your power, push beyond your comfort zone, and embrace the audacious spirit within you. The path to growth is not always easy, but it is always worth it.

Remember, audacious expansion is not about grand gestures or dramatic transformations. It's about the small, daily choices you make to move forward, to trust in your potential, and to create a life that aligns with your deepest values and aspirations. It's about the courage to take action, even when the outcome is uncertain.

Your expansion story isn't just about where you've been—it's about where you're going. You're creating a roadmap for others to follow. The most powerful expansion happens when you choose it, when you decide to grow not because circumstances demand it, but because your audacious spirit calls you forward.

Your story is still being written. Make it one worth telling.

EXPANSION IN ACTION CHALLENGE

This week, step into your expansion story with these three steps:

1. **Audacious History Timeline:** Create a personal timeline of the 3-5 most significant expansions you've already made in your life. For each expansion point, note what pushed you to expand, what fears you overcame, and what growth resulted. Keep this visible as a reminder that you are already an expansion expert with proven capacity to stretch.

2. **Authentic Leadership Inventory:** Identify three areas where you've been "wearing khakis" instead of showing up authentically. For each area, determine one small but meaningful step you can take this week to bring more of your authentic self forward. Challenge yourself to make at least one of these steps visible to others who might benefit from seeing your example.

3. **Barrier-Breaking Plan:** Select one professional or personal barrier you've been hesitant to challenge. Break it down into three increasingly bold action steps. Commit to completing the first step within 48 hours, regardless of how uncomfortable it feels. Document both the action and your feelings before and after taking it.

SHARE YOUR JOURNEY

✺ "I'm embracing my expansion story by [specific action from your challenges]. Every time we stretch beyond our comfort zone, we create a new baseline for what's possible. What boundaries are you breaking to live more authentically today? #AudaciousExpansion"

Part 5:

YOUR EXPANDING LEGACY

Don't forget to download your free journal before continuing.

Chapter 20:

SETBACKS ARE SETUPS IN DISGUISE

Setbacks are not failures. They are redirections, invitations, and sacred pauses built into the journey.

Building a legacy isn't a straight line from vision to victory. The most powerful legacies—the ones that truly change lives and create lasting impact—are forged through struggle and refined by the courage to keep going when everything falls apart.

As we talk about expanding into your legacy, we have to acknowledge this truth: setbacks are not obstacles to your expansion—they're integral to it. They're not detours from your path—they ARE the path.

The most meaningful impact doesn't always come from our victories, but also from how we handle our defeats. How we rise after falling. How we help others navigate their own storms because we've weathered our own. This is why understanding setbacks is crucial to expanding your legacy—because your setbacks become someone else's breakthrough when you share how you moved through them.

Throughout this book, we've discussed setbacks in various contexts. However, I felt it was crucial to dedicate an entire chapter to this topic, so that when you encounter obstacles on your journey, you can turn to this specific chapter for guidance and reassurance.

Setbacks are not just about the present moment; they are opportunities for growth and learning that will shape your future. By diving deep into the subject of setbacks, we can equip ourselves with the tools and mindset necessary to navigate challenges and emerge stronger, wiser, and more resilient.

Setbacks are never on our vision board. No one pins "loss," "burnout," "failure," or "that season where everything felt too much and not enough" on their dream wall. But the setbacks come anyway. Sometimes in whispers. Sometimes like a freight train.

I've stood in mud-covered boots on construction sites, knowing I was building more than a structure—I was building a life. I've worn heels in boardrooms and still carried the weight of being "mom" in my bones. There have been seasons where my success was louder than my soul, and others where

I looked around and wondered if I'd traded too much for too little.

Setbacks are the moments that strip you bare. They humble your hustle. They remind you that no matter how strong your systems, sometimes life just happens. And when it does, it doesn't ask for your permission.

But setbacks aren't signs to stop. They're invitations to shift. To adjust. To pause.

We all encounter those reality checks that force us to think deeply. Maybe we feel like we're on the wrong path. Maybe we're stuck in mud, not moving anywhere. Or perhaps it's like we're in quicksand—the world is moving so fast around us that despite our efforts, we feel stagnant.

This chapter is to remind you that we all have those moments. Most people aren't posting about them; most people aren't even telling you about them. Most people are not clapping or applauding for the people that say "I need to take the pause," "I need to take the time out," or "I may just not be in that season to audaciously and fully expand right now."

Audaciously expanding, just like anything else that needs to expand, needs time to heal, needs time to grow, and needs time to breathe.

THE SACRED PAUSE

Legacy isn't built in one season. It's layered—over years, over growth spurts (mine and my kids'), over pivots, pauses, and powerful comebacks. There are bright stages of light—where you feel seen, valued, and alive. There are dim stages—when the spotlight moves and you're not sure who you are outside of the titles you carry.

We love the idea of forward motion—the bold step, the visible win, the big leap. But what we often forget is that expansion is not all spotlight moments and perfectly timed breakthroughs.

Sometimes, expansion looks like stillness. Like silence. Like stumbling, recalibrating, or even sitting it out for a season. Setbacks don't mean you're behind—they mean you're becoming.

There will be seasons when you can show up fully—front and center, hands-on, heart-forward. And there will be seasons when your power is quiet. When the boldest thing you can do is rest, grieve, heal, or wait. That's still action. That's still brave.

Expansion isn't just about the fire. It's also about the ashes. It's about what you build in the rebuilding. What you find in the undoing. What you hear in the quiet.

These are what I call sacred pauses—the moments when life invites us to slow down, to reflect, and to reconnect with ourselves and our purpose.

What's important for me to remember is that I only get my kids this age once. There's no replay button for their messy middle school days, their early morning football games, their heartfelt questions on the ride home from practice.

My daughter's hand still fits in mine today. One day it won't. And my legacy? It's not just what I build out in the world. It's what I build within the walls of my home—in the quiet moments that don't get posted but stay etched in their memory.

I've had to gut-check my own vision more than once. Not because I'm not dreaming big, but because I refuse to build a life so big that it forgets the little things.

When we're in the midst of a sacred pause, it's easy to feel like we're stuck or falling behind. We may compare ourselves to others who seem to be leaping ahead, or we may feel pressure to "get back on track" as quickly as possible. But what if we approached these pauses not as obstacles, but as opportunities?

Sacred pauses give us the space to ask important questions: Am I moving in a direction that aligns with my values and purpose? What do I need to release or realign in order to keep growing? How can I use this moment to deepen my self-awareness and resilience?

Think about any type of animal. How long does it take before they're ready to enter the world? Think about any person who's training for that bike race. They don't just go out and ride that hundred miles. It takes the rest, it takes the pauses, and sometimes it means that right now you're not ready to run the race.

Respect that. Honor that, embrace that and recognize that's part of your story. Part of being audacious, part of being in the space that you need to be in.

We don't get to choose all the timing. Sometimes, you're called to plant seeds in the dark—when you're tired, uncertain, or afraid. But even in those moments, something is growing. Maybe not in the world's eyes, but in your soul. Your legacy gets built in those tiny, unseen acts of love, leadership, and courage.

It's okay if your stage looks different right now. It's okay if expansion feels quiet, still, or slower than you imagined. You're not behind. You're just building something real.

This chapter is also my reminder that we never know what anyone's going through. We never know what's happening behind closed doors. We need to slow down to also recognize the importance of giving other people the grace they deserve. We need to give them a second chance. We need to give them the opportunity to have their season and their space.

All too often we assume everything's okay from the outside—from that glossy Instagram story—but we never know what someone's struggling with inside. Grace is a mirror. If we're not giving it to ourselves, we're likely not giving it to others either. When we learn to treat ourselves with kindness and understanding, we naturally begin to offer the same to those around us.

Maybe it's a family member, a friend, a business partner, or even a stranger. Whoever it is, let's give ourselves and others the grace and kindness we all deserve.

Your audacious expansion requires these moments. They shape you. They sharpen you. They slow you down just enough to make sure you're growing in the right direction.

Sometimes it's because of these setbacks, because of these pauses, that we later discover the significance behind our struggles. When we look back—whether it's next season or years from now—we realize that everything happened for a very specific reason. We don't always see it in the moment, but in hindsight, it's so clear how every detour led us exactly where we needed to be.

So if you're in a season that feels paused, heavy, or off-track, know this: You are still expanding. Even here. *Especially* here.

As you read this, think about your own expansion. Where are you right now? Be honest with yourself. Let it sink in. Stop worrying about the person to your right or left, the person in front of you, or even the person behind you who might need your grace.

Wherever you're at, let's give ourselves the space to breathe. The space to say, "I'm still expanding, I'm still growing. Just because I'm not checking every box doesn't mean I'm not making progress."

Even in a sacred pause, you are exactly where you need to be. Trust the process, lean into the discomfort, and know that this moment and your perceived setback is actually a setup for your most audacious becoming yet.

AUDACITY IN ACTION CHALLENGE

This week, practice honoring your current season while extending grace to yourself and others:

1. **Season Assessment:** Take fifteen minutes to honestly assess what season you're in right now. Are you in a growth phase, a rest phase, or a transition phase?

Write down what this season requires of you and what it's teaching you. Honor where you are instead of where you think you should be.

2. **Grace Practice:** Identify one area where you've been harsh with yourself for not progressing fast enough. Replace self-criticism with self-compassion by writing yourself a letter of encouragement, acknowledging your efforts and growth even in the slow seasons.

3. **Extend Grace to Others:** Think of someone in your life who might be struggling or in a difficult season. Reach out with a simple message of support or encouragement, without trying to fix or rush their process.

SHARE YOUR JOURNEY

✸ "I'm learning that expansion isn't always about growing bigger—sometimes it's about growing deeper, resting well, and honoring the season I'm in. What season are you in, and how are you honoring it? #AudaciousExpansion"

Chapter 21:

LIVING OUT LOUD (FINALLY)

*You don't owe anyone the old version
of you if it's not serving you.*

Are you ready to embrace the power of living out loud? It's time to take a bold new approach, even if it means stepping outside your comfort zone.

We often find ourselves stuck in familiar patterns, clinging to what's comfortable because it's what we know. But audaciously expanding means being willing to say no to what no longer serves us. It might mean shutting down a business that isn't working, or making more time for your rapidly growing children by letting go of unfulfilling commitments.

Ask yourself: What does growth look like for you? How do you need to expand and evolve to create the life you truly desire?

If you haven't noticed by now, audacious expansion is not a formula. It's not a scientific method. It's not A plus B equals C. Sometimes it's the crazy route. Sometimes it's three steps backward that take you ten steps ahead. It's a lens through which to evaluate and approach your life. That's why there are so many different approaches to expanding audaciously.

Maybe you're feeling stuck in a situation that should have been a stepping stone to your expansion, but fear is holding you back from making a change. You might be thinking, "What if I take a risk and it doesn't work out?"

Well, let me ask you this: Is it going to feel safe five, ten, fifteen years from now if you stay exactly where you are just because it was comfortable today?

Are you willing to take the challenge?

Living out loud means being willing to let go of what no longer serves you, even if it's familiar or comfortable. It means being honest with yourself about what you truly want and need, and taking bold action to align your life with your deepest values and aspirations.

When we live out loud, we give ourselves permission to grow, evolve, and expand in ways that may feel uncertain at first. We let go of the need to cling to old identities, roles, or commitments that no longer fit who we are becoming. Instead, we embrace the journey of authentic self-expression and trust that by being true to ourselves, we will attract the people, opportunities, and experiences that are aligned with our highest potential.

Living out loud is not about being perfect or having it all figured out. It's about being willing to take risks, to be vulnerable, and to show up fully as yourself in all aspects of your life. It's about letting go of the masks and facades that keep you playing small and instead embracing the beauty and power of your authentic self.

So, if you find yourself at a point where something needs to change, where you feel called to expand in new and exciting ways, I invite you to consider: What would it look like to start living out loud? What parts of yourself have you been hiding or holding back, and what might become possible if you were to embrace and express them fully?

Maybe living out loud means speaking up about an issue that matters deeply to you, even if it means ruffling some feathers. Maybe it means pursuing a creative passion or starting a business that aligns with your values, even if others don't understand or support your vision at first. Or maybe it simply means being more honest and authentic in your relationships, even if it feels vulnerable or uncomfortable. The question is: Will staying where you are get you where you need to go?

Remember, you don't owe anyone the old version of you if it's not serving your growth and well-being. Embracing your authentic self in this season of life is a crucial part of living fully and expanding audaciously.

THE REAL TALK ABOUT LIVING FULLY

And while we're talking about living fully, let's get real about the stuff that actually keeps us awake at 3 AM—the conversations we have in our heads but never out loud. The truths that make us feel like we're the only ones struggling with this messy, beautiful expansion.

Money. Let's start there because it's the elephant in every room. You know that sick feeling in your stomach when you have to negotiate your salary? That voice that whispers you should be grateful for what you have instead of asking for more? That's not humility—that's conditioning. We've been taught that good women don't chase money, don't demand their worth, don't talk numbers at dinner parties.

But your financial freedom isn't selfish—it's survival. It's the difference between choosing your life and having your life chosen for you. When you can't afford to leave the job that's draining you, when you can't take risks because you're living paycheck to paycheck, when you're one emergency away from financial crisis—that's not being responsible, that's being trapped.

I've watched too many brilliant women stay small financially because they were uncomfortable asking for what they're worth. They'll research every detail about a vacation but won't negotiate their salary. They'll advocate fiercely for their kids but whisper when it comes to their own compensation.

Your audacious expansion includes getting uncomfortable about money. Learning to say "I'm worth more" without apologizing. Tracking your spending not to shame yourself, but to understand where your money actually goes. Investing in yourself—whether that's education, coaching, or starting that side business. Building wealth that gives you options, not just security. Because when you control your money, you control your choices.

Your body. The one that's carried you through everything and somehow you still criticize in the mirror. Perimenopause hits and suddenly your metabolism laughs at your old strategies. Your sex drive shifts. Your sleep patterns change. Your energy isn't what it used to be. The jeans that fit last year mock you from the closet.

And instead of honoring this transition, we panic. We chase the bodies we had at 25, the energy we had before kids, the libido we had in our honeymoon phase. We buy the supplements, try the diets, push ourselves harder at the gym, wondering why nothing works like it used to.

Your audacious expansion includes radical self-acceptance of where you are right now. It means having the hard conversations with your partner about what you need. It means saying no to things that drain you and yes to things that restore you.

Maybe that means working with a trainer who understands your life stage. Maybe it's finally addressing the sleep issues you've been ignoring. Maybe it's hormone therapy that lets you feel like yourself again. Maybe it's giving yourself permission to rest without guilt. Your body has been your most faithful companion—it's time to treat it like one.

Relationships and intimacy. The stuff nobody talks about at book club. How expansion can threaten people around you. How success can make your partner uncomfortable. How your growth can expose the places where your relationships aren't growing with you.

Guess what? Not everyone will celebrate your growth. Some people were comfortable with the smaller version of you. When you start setting boundaries, speaking up, or pursuing dreams you'd put on hold, it can shake the foundation of relationships that were built on your people-pleasing.

You can love someone deeply and still outgrow the dynamic you've built together. You can be grateful for your marriage and still want more conversation, more intimacy, more adventure, more depth. Wanting more doesn't make you ungrateful—it makes you human.

The hardest part? Learning to say what you actually need instead of what you think people want to hear. "I need more support with the kids." "I need you to plan date nights sometimes." "I need space to pursue this dream." These conversations can save relationships or end them, and both outcomes can be exactly what's needed.

The mental load. That invisible weight of remembering everything, planning everything, anticipating everyone's needs while your own get pushed to the bottom of an endless list. You know what I'm talking about—the mental spreadsheet that runs 24/7 in your head. Soccer practice at 4, grocery list, mom's birthday next week, dog needs shots, kids need new shoes, anniversary is coming up, did I pay the electric bill?

It's the exhaustion that comes not just from doing everything, but from thinking about everything. The way you can feel completely overwhelmed and completely invisible at the same time. How you can be the CEO of your household but feel like nobody sees the thousand tiny decisions you make every day.

Your audacious expansion includes redistributing this load. It means having conversations about the invisible work you do. It means teaching your partner to notice when the toilet paper is running low instead of just replacing it when you ask. It means setting boundaries around your mental energy and refusing to be the default solution to everyone else's problems.

Maybe that looks like a family calendar everyone can see. Maybe it's delegating real responsibility, not just tasks. Maybe it's saying "I don't know, what do you think?" when someone asks you to solve their problem. Maybe it's taking that weekend away without leaving a detailed instruction manual.

These aren't side conversations to your expansion—they're the foundation. Remember the triangle from chapter 7? You can't build an audacious life on a shaky financial foundation, in a body you're at war with, in relationships that require you to stay small, while carrying the weight of everyone else's world on your shoulders.

Whatever form it takes, living out loud is an essential part of the audacious expansion process. It is a way of claiming your space in the world, of owning your unique gifts and talents, and of inspiring others to do the same. When you live out loud, you become a beacon of possibility and a catalyst for positive change.

So, if you're ready to take a new approach and embrace the power of living out loud, know that you have everything you need within you to create a life that is authentic, fulfilling, and expansive. And know that by being true to yourself and shining your light, you are making a difference in the world simply by being who you are.

As painful as it was, that punch woke me up. It showed me the places I had been playing small, where I had wrapped myself in survival instead of standing in my full expansion. It cracked me open, and through that crack, the light got in. I don't want you to wait for your punch. Don't wait to be knocked down to wake up. Use my punch as your permission slip—as your energy and your sign—that *now* is your moment.

Throughout this book, I've shared real, tangible tools to help you move through the thick of it: how to recognize where you've been limiting yourself, how to find security within when everything outside feels shaky, and how to say yes to your next level, even when it's scary. The universe sends invitations in the most unexpected, often messy ways—and what's waiting on the other side of your transformation makes every hard moment worth it.

I don't want to do this alone. I want to create a movement. I want to be the catalyst. I want to be the seed. I want to be the spark and the light for so many women who have watched my journey, so many women whose journeys I've watched, who have been a catalyst in my life.

That's why in 2025, I launched my first Audacious Women's Summit—the first of many. It's a space where women can unlock their true potential, a safe haven where authenticity and audacity thrive. Picture a room filled with people who are unapologetically themselves, who embrace their expansive nature. Imagine women standing on tables, cheering each other on with unwavering support. Hand in hand, we'll help one another step into the versions of ourselves we've always been meant to be.

AUDACIOUS WOMEN'S SUMMIT

Living your expanded life isn't something that happens once. It's not a destination you reach and then relax. It's a daily practice, a constant becoming. It's about waking up each morning and choosing expansion over contraction, authenticity over approval, courage over comfort.

What if your "too much" was never a flaw, but the beginning of your audacious expansion? What if the very thing you were told to dim was actually your power, your light, your purpose asking to be seen?

Taking up space isn't arrogance—it's alignment. It's embodying your joy, your truth, your fire and letting it overflow into every room you walk into.

You were never meant to shrink. You were meant to rise, to radiate, to root down *and* reach wide—like wildflowers after the storm. Bold. Beautiful. Uncontainable.

The world doesn't need your quiet compliance. It needs your full, free, audacious self.

EXPANSION IN ACTION CHALLENGE

This week, commit to living your expanded life with these three steps:

1. **Legacy Letter:** Write a letter from your future self (one, five, or ten years from now) to your present self, describing the expanded life you're living and the impact you've had. Be specific about what you've accomplished, how you show up in the world, and the legacy you're actively creating. Include details about the areas where you've been most audacious in your choices. After writing, identify three specific actions you can take this week that align with this future vision.

2. **Unedited Authenticity Practice:** Choose three interactions this week where you will practice showing up with complete authenticity. Before each interaction, set an intention to let go of the filters, masks, or performance aspects you typically employ. Afterward, journal about what felt different, what surprised you, and what became possible when you showed up unedited.

3. **Expansion Ripple Map:** Create a visual representation of how your expansion creates ripples that impact others. Start with yourself in the center, then draw concentric circles representing your immediate family, friends, colleagues, community, and beyond. For each circle, identify at least one way your audacious choices have already inspired or could inspire others to expand. Be specific about the permission your expansion gives to those around you.

SHARE YOUR JOURNEY

✪ "I'm living my expanded life by [specific action from your challenges]. Our legacies aren't just what we leave behind— they're how we live right now. How are you creating your legacy today? #AudaciousExpansion"

Chapter 22

WRITE YOUR OWN DAMN ENDING

Life can change in a heartbeat... but in that shattering,
something else gets revealed: the unbreakable
core of who you are.

What if the most audacious act isn't climbing a mountain or starting a company, but simply deciding—truly deciding— to become the person you were meant to be? What if your greatest expansion isn't waiting somewhere in the future, but is available to you right now, in this moment, through the choices you make today?

As we reach these final pages together, I want to challenge your conception of what comes next. Your audacious future isn't some distant horizon you'll eventually reach—it's unfolding with each breath you take, each decision you make, each time you choose expansion over contraction.

Nine hundred and ninety-nine days. That's how long it took from the moment I was assaulted to the day I stood in a courtroom to deliver my victim statement. Nearly three years of waiting, wondering, and wrestling with the aftermath of trauma.

Through those dark days, I learned the true meaning of the audacity to be resilient—a message I now share in my keynote speeches. It's about deciding how we'll let our challenges shape us. Will we allow the punches thrown our way to refine us or define us? Will we let tragedy shatter our spirits or use it as a foundation to build something greater? Can we find the strength to transform setbacks into setups, to see obstacles as opportunities for growth?

Standing in that courtroom, I shared these words:

"I vividly remember thinking that, before the strangulation, it might be the last moment I'd ever be a mom to my two young kids, the last time I'd be a wife, and perhaps my final breath as a living person on this earth... But I am reminded by Maya Angelou, 'I can be changed by what happened to me. But I refuse to be reduced by it.' Staying quiet or scared has never been my mission in life."

That punch taught me that life can change in a heartbeat. In one terrifying moment, everything you think you know about safety, about control, about tomorrow being guaranteed gets shattered. But in that shattering, something else gets revealed: the unbreakable core of who you are.

THE POWER OF NOW

That day in court, I stood not just as a survivor but as a speaker, a leader, wife, an advocate, and a mother. We all face hardships—"punches"—in both our professional and personal lives, but what truly matters is what we do with them—how we rise, how we lead, and how we create change. That moment crystallized why my message matters. Why I stand on stages. Why I speak out.

The physical wounds healed, but the internal transformation became the raw material for expansion. It became the fuel for everything I'm sharing with you right now.

So let me ask you something, and I want you to really sit with this: Imagine what you would do with no fear, no limitations, no impostor syndrome whispering in your ear. Imagine what your life could look like. Not just tomorrow, but the feeling you could experience every morning when you wake up. Imagine how you would feel ten, twenty, thirty years from now because you bet on yourself.

The truth is, you don't get unlimited chances. You don't get endless dress rehearsals. Life is happening *RIGHT NOW.*

You said yes to that thing that felt so scary. Yes to that thing that allowed you to expand. Yes to that thing that put you in such an uncomfortable spot, yet was exactly what you needed to unlock your potential. What is that thing for you? Close your eyes and imagine who you can become. Imagine who you are beneath the layers of doubt and hesitation. Imagine the legacy that you can ultimately leave.

As I planned my first Audacious Women's Summit, I confronted these same questions. Imagine if I had decided it was too much work, that I didn't have the resources or funding, that I had no idea if anyone would show up. But then imagine the alternative—saying yes, as I ultimately did. Packing a room with 170 women, selling out the event, securing vendors and sponsors, having people there rooting me on and literally starting a ripple impact.

This summit represents everything I believe about audacious expansion—that it's not a solitary journey but a collective movement. That when one of us expands, we create permission for others to do the same. That our individual audacity, when joined together, becomes an unstoppable force for change.

The truth about expansion is that it requires a willingness to be uncomfortable, to look foolish, to stand apart. She who expands must be willing to be uncertain, to pivot, to invest, to be criticized (a lot), to begin again, to contradict herself in public, to let go of immediate gratification, to release old identities and even old relationships, to do things scared, to fall on her face, to get back up, and to love herself even when others don't. There is no instant pot of gold waiting for us—expansion requires consistent work. Luck, as they say, is what happens when preparation meets opportunity.

We all wear many hats. Sometimes we feel like no matter which hat we put on, we just aren't enough. But expansion isn't about wearing every hat—it's about choosing the *right* hat for the part of the journey you're on. Maybe your expansion means putting on one hat and taking off two others. Maybe it means adding new ones. In my own life, I've tried to juggle too many hats at once, only to wear none of them well. Expansion is about discernment: who you need to be right now, and what deserves your yes.

So what areas of your life need expansion? Where are you letting that inner voice—the impostor syndrome, the critic to your right or left—tell you no? I think back to my own doubts: wondering as a child if I'd ever learn to read, wondering as a teenager if I'd ever be loved, wondering as a young engineer if I belonged in a male-dominated field, wondering if I deserved a seat in the boardroom, wondering if I deserved a microphone on stage. And yet every single one of those doubts became an invitation to expand.

That's why I asked you earlier to create your *Audacious Badass List*—your inventory of ways you've already grown. Go back to it. Let it remind you how far you've come, and how much further you can still go.

Don't forget the other essential tools for navigating audacious expansion—your blueprint, your compass, and your BOLD vision. These concepts have been woven into every chapter, guiding you toward a life of purpose, resilience, and authentic self-expression.

You are capable of extraordinary things. You are not too small. You are enough. The person ahead of you doesn't necessarily have more skills or resources. The difference is you. You are the differentiating factor. You alone can decide to expand.

And maybe that's why it feels so right to close this book on Chapter 22. The number 22 has been a thread throughout my life, appearing in moments of significant growth, change, and transformation. It's a number that, for me, represents the power of personal expansion—the ability to stretch beyond our perceived limits and create lives of purpose, joy, and authentic self-expression.

9/22: My Wedding Anniversary

7/22: Drew's birthday, Adelyn is 8/11 (1+1)

8/22: My sister's anniversary & my first friend Amy's birthday

222: The last 3 digits of my phone number

422: Isagenix legacy number

22: Drew's football number

22: My old soccer number

2022: The year of the attack (and my audacious expansion)

222: The last official page in this book

I finally tattooed it on my skin because it wouldn't stop showing up. In numerology, 22 is called the "master builder"—a symbol of balance, resilience, and the power to turn vision into reality. To me, 22 is alignment. It is audacity. It is expansion.

Ending on Chapter 22 is an intention. Because being intentional is what leads to expansion. It's my way of saying that expansion isn't just something I teach. It's something I live. And now it's your invitation to live it too.

Every single day is made up of tiny moments where you get to choose expansion over contraction. Every conversation. Every decision. Every time you choose courage over comfort. Every time you say yes when fear screams no. Those 999 days of healing taught me that we don't get infinite chances. We get today. We get this moment. We get right now.

So let me ask you: If your life ended tomorrow, would you leave this earth having expressed your truest self? Would you leave behind your legacy? Would you depart having lived your biggest expansion?

Your audacious future isn't far away. It's being written now, in the choices you make today.

You don't need permission. You don't need a perfect plan. You don't need all the answers. You just need the audacity to begin. Your audacious future—and everyone whose life you're meant to touch—is counting on your decision.

The world has been waiting long enough, and I can't wait to watch you crush it.

Here's the thing: The movement doesn't end when you close this book. *This is where everything truly begins.*

The ripples of your expansion will keep flowing long after you've turned the last page—touching lives, inspiring change, creating possibility for people who need to see someone like you deciding to go all-in on themselves.

It's time to break free from the limitations that have been holding you back and create the ultimate, authentic life that's been waiting for you to say yes.

Choose expansion. Choose courage. Choose YOU.

EXPANSION IN ACTION CHALLENGE

This week, step into your audacious future with these three steps:

1. **Vision Creation:** Dedicate 60 uninterrupted minutes to creating a detailed vision of your life. Unlike traditional goal-setting, focus on how you will feel, who you will be, and the impact you'll be having—not just what you'll achieve. Write this in present tense as if you're already there. Include specific details about how you're showing up in your relationships, work, health, and community. Place this vision somewhere you'll see it daily and commit to reading it aloud each morning for the next month.

2. **Movement Commitment:** Identify three people in your circle who would benefit from your expansion message. Schedule a meaningful conversation with each of them in the next two weeks to share what you've learned and how you're applying it.

3. **Future-Self Installation:** Create a "future-self ritual" that you'll practice daily for the next thirty days. This could be as simple as spending five minutes each morning embodying the energy, posture, and mindset

of your most expanded self before beginning your day. Make it tangible with a physical anchor—perhaps a special piece of jewelry, a particular spot in your home, or a specific phrase you say to yourself. This practice bridges the gap between who you are now and who you're becoming.

SHARE YOUR JOURNEY

✺ "I'm creating my audacious future by [specific action from your challenges]. The future isn't something that happens to us—it's something we create with each bold choice. What audacious step are you taking today? #AudaciousExpansion

Want More?

GRIT GRACE & GLITZ PODCAST

THE AUDACIOUS BOOTCAMP MASTERMIND

AUDACIOUS WOMEN'S SUMMIT

Let me Acknowledge You

To write a book like this takes guts, grit, and grace — but it also takes a village. And wow, what a village I've had.

First and foremost, to my husband, Andrew — thank you for being the steady rock behind my whirlwind ideas. For believing in this book (and me) on the early mornings, the late nights, and the messy-in-between moments. You never once blinked at the chaos — you just said, go for it. Your support was oxygen to this dream.

To Drew and Adelyn — my reason, my why, my everyday miracles. You remind me daily what audacious expansion looks like whether it's on the football field, on the dance stage, or in the quiet, courageous moments of your lives. Watching you grow into who you are has pushed me to grow into who I'm meant to be. I hope this book becomes a blueprint you can one day hold close.

To my sister, Kimberly — you've always marched to your own drum, and because of that, you've taught me to do the same. Your authenticity and fierce loyalty have been a lighthouse for me.

To my mom — thank you for planting roots so deep I've never forgotten where I come from, and wings so strong I've never been afraid to fly.

To my dad — you taught me something foundational: to invest in myself first. That lesson learned, raw, real, gave me strength I never knew I had.

To the friends who've become family, how do I even begin? You've held my hand through storms, cheered me on when I forgot how to cheer for myself, and reminded me of who I am when life tried to make me forget. Whether we connected in a boardroom, on a beach, at a business retreat, or over a frantic voice note or late-night text, please know this: your belief in me helped me turn thoughts into chapters, and chapters into this book.

You know who you are. If you're reading this, it's probably because you were meant to.

To every bold, brave soul who whispered "keep going" — thank you.

Your encouragement helped me fly higher than I thought possible.

And above all, to God and the Universe, thank you for the divine nudges, the soul whispers, the well-timed signs, and the unwavering presence. When I doubted, you redirected. When I paused, you pushed. When I questioned, you answered in subtle miracles and giant reminders.

This book was never just mine. It's all of ours: every tear, every triumph, every breadcrumb along the way.

Thank you for walking this path with me.

Let's keep expanding. Audaciously.

About the Author

From steel-toed boots to global stages, Erika Rothenberger has been breaking molds and building momentum for over two decades. With a hard hat in one hand and a mic in the other, she's the unapologetically bold force behind Audacious Expansion—a movement, a mindset, and now, a book.

A high-impact leader in the construction industry, Erika serves as Director of Performance Systems for a national utility contractor. She holds credentials as a LEED AP and PMP, and brings her engineering expertise and business acumen to every boardroom she enters. But her story doesn't stop there.

As a keynote speaker, bestselling author, podcaster, and wellness entrepreneur, Erika empowers women to rise with grit, grace, and audacity. She's delivered her signature frameworks on leadership, connection, and resilience to audiences across the country, blending real-life stories with powerful strategies. Her 170+ episode podcast, Grit, Grace & Glitz, is a beacon for ambitious women carving their own path.

A survivor turned advocate, Erika's journey took a life-altering turn in 2022 when she was attacked in a workplace parking lot. Instead of shrinking, she rose—turning pain into purpose, launching community spaces for healing and growth, and becoming a voice for women navigating challenge, change, and comeback.

Erika is the founder of two female empowerment networks, a Board member and Co-Chair of the Executive Roundtable with POWER, and host of the Audacious Women's Summit—a full-day transformational event coming to the Greater Philadelphia area. (Learn more at: www.erikarothenberger.com/audacious-womens-summit)

When she's not speaking, writing, or mentoring, Erika is chasing sunsets with her husband Andy and their two incredible kids, Drew and Adelyn, in Harleysville, PA. Whether she's on the football field sidelines or watching a dance recital, or traveling the world she knows the truest legacy she's building is the one her children get to live alongside her.

Erika believes that women aren't meant to fit in boxes—they're meant to break them wide open. She's here to help others do the same. So, if you're ready to lead, rise, and expand into the boldest version of yourself—Erika is already cheering you on.

Linkedin: @erikarothenberger
Instagram: @erikalearothenberger
Website: www.erikarothenberger.com
Podcast: Grit, Grace & Glitz (available on all platforms)

CHAPTER 5: TRUE NORTH OR BUST

1. Apple Inc. "Think Different" Advertisement Campaign. TBWA\Chiat\Day, 1997.
2. Jobs, Steve. Interview with Santa Clara Valley Historical Association, 1995.

CHAPTER 8: DITCH BUSY. CHOOSE ABUNDANCE.

1. Scheier, Michael F., and Charles S. Carver. "Optimism, Coping, and Health: Assessment and Implications of Generalized Outcome Expectancies." Health Psychology 4, no. 3 (1985): 219-247.
2. Dweck, Carol S. Mindset: The New Psychology of Success. New York: Random House, 2006.
3. Blackwell, Lisa S., Kali H. Trzesniewski, and Carol S. Dweck. "Implicit Theories of Intelligence Predict

Achievement Across an Adolescent Transition: A Longitudinal Study and an Intervention." Child Development 78, no. 1 (2007): 246-263.

4. Mani, Anandi, Sendhil Mullainathan, Eldar Shafir, and Jiaying Zhao. "Poverty Impedes Cognitive Function." Science 341, no. 6149 (2013): 976-980.

5. Shah, Anuj K., Sendhil Mullainathan, and Eldar Shafir. "Some Consequences of Having Too Little." Science 338, no. 6107 (2012): 682-685.

6. McCullough, Michael E., Robert A. Emmons, and Jo-Ann Tsang. "The Grateful Disposition: A Conceptual and Empirical Topography." Journal of Personality and Social Psychology 82, no. 1 (2002): 112-127.

7. Robbins, Mel. Let Them: A Little Guide to Not Taking It Personally. Carlsbad, CA: Hay House, 2024.

8. Mark, Gloria, Daniela Gudith, and Ulrich Klocke. "The Cost of Interrupted Work: More Speed and Stress." CHI '08 Proceedings (2008): 107-110.

9. Psychology Today. "98 Percent of People Can't Multitask ... 2 Percent of People Can Juggle Without ... Ill Effects." February 24, 2012.

10. Willink, Jocko. Discipline Equals Freedom: Field Manual. New York: St. Martin's Press, 2017.

11. Financial Poise. "72% of Workers Who Aren't Working in Their Dream Job Regret It." February 18, 2025.

12. Davidai, Shai, and Thomas Gilovich. "The Ideal Road Not Taken: The Self-Discrepancies Involved in People's Most Enduring Regrets." Emotion 18, no. 3 (2018): 400-415.

CHAPTER 9: CRUSH THE CAGES; OPEN YOUR CIRCLE

1. Aaker, Jennifer. "Stories Are Remembered Up to 22 Times More Than Facts Alone." Stanford Graduate School of Business Women's Leadership Center. Accessed September 5, 2025.
2. Lima, Jamie Kern. WORTHY: How to Believe You Are Enough and Transform Your Life. Carlsbad, CA: Hay House, 2025.
3. Psychology Today. "Core Beliefs Are Formed in Childhood Before Age 7." September 13, 2021.

CHAPTER 10: UNFOLLOW TO FLY

1. Asurion. "Americans Now Check Their Phones 96 Times a Day -- That's Once Every 10 Minutes." Press release, November 21, 2019.
2. MasterMind Behavior. "Average Screen Time Statistics." MasterMindBehavior.com, March 3, 2025.
3. "Social Media Mental Health Statistics 2025." ElectroIQ, accessed 9/02/2025. "60% of social media users say it negatively affects their self-esteem." https://electroiq.com/stats/social-media-mental-health-statistics/

4. Lago, Amberly. *Joy Through the Journey: Shift Your Mindset, Embrace the Present Moment, and Cultivate Resilience Through Life's Ups and Downs.* Hoboken, NJ: John Wiley & Sons, 2025.

CHAPTER 13: OWN YOUR OWN FLAVOR OF CRAZY

1. Clear, James. *Atomic Habits: An Easy & Proven Way to Build Good Habits & Break Bad Ones.* New York: Avery, 2018.

CHAPTER 14: CIRCLE UP, LEVEL UP

1. Waldinger, Robert, and Marc Schulz. *The Good Life: Lessons from the World's Longest Scientific Study of Happiness.* New York: Simon & Schuster, 2023.
2. Stanford Center for Compassion and Altruism Research and Education. "Connectedness & Health: The Science of Social Connection." Stanford University, 2013.

CHAPTER 16: PLANS WITH SWAGGER

1. Huffington, Arianna. *Thrive: The Third Metric to Redefining Success and Creating a Life of Well-*

Being, Wisdom, and Wonder. New York: Harmony Books, 2014.

2. Breslin, Mark. The Five Minute Foreman: Mastering the People Side of Construction. San Francisco: Breslin Strategies, 2013.

3. Collins, Jim. Good to Great: Why Some Companies Make the Leap... and Others Don't. New York: HarperCollins, 2001.

CHAPTER 17: FUEL UP ON FEAR

1. Harteneck, Patricia. "Negative Self-Talk: Don't Let It Overwhelm You." Psychology Today, December 14, 2017.

2. Poynter Institute. "CNN Will Cut Back on Its Broken 'Breaking News.'" Poynter Commentary, June 3, 2022.

3. LaFreniere, Lucas S., and Michelle G. Newman. "Exposing Worry's Deceit: Percentage of Untrue Worries in Generalized Anxiety Disorder Treatment." Behavior Therapy (2020), cited in Seth J. Gillihan, "How Often Do Your Worries Actually Come True?" Psychology Today, July 19, 2019.

4. Brown, H. Jackson Jr. P.S. I Love You. Nashville: Rutledge Hill Press, 1990.

5. Shelton, Trent. Protect Your Peace: Nine Unapologetic Principles for Thriving in a Chaotic World. Los Angeles: Hay House, 2024.

CHAPTER 18: HELL YES OR HARD NO

1. Robbins, Mel. "What Is the Let Them Theory?" The Mel Robbins Podcast, episode 119. Accessed September 8, 2025.

CHAPTER 19: BOUNCE BACK LIKE A BOSS

1. McEwen, Bruce S. "Protective and Damaging Effects of Stress Mediators." New England Journal of Medicine 338, no. 3 (1998): 171-179.
2. Schultz, Wolfram. "Multiple Reward Signals in the Brain." Nature Reviews Neuroscience 1, no. 3 (2000): 199-207.
3. Barrett, Lisa Feldman. Seven and a Half Lessons About the Brain. New York: Houghton Mifflin Harcourt, 2020.